LIFE'S A TRIP:

Watch for God's Lessons along the Way

"…cause me to know the way wherein I should walk…"
- Psalm 143:8

TARVAH MCGINTY

ALETHEIA PRESS

Unless otherwise indicated, Scripture quotations are taken from the KING JAMES VERSION (KJV): KING JAMES VERSION, public domain.

Published by Aletheia Press, LLC
Houston, TX
www.aletheiapressbooks.com

Printed in the United States of America

Print ISBN: 9798391990222

A note from the author about the cover: "I chose this picture as the cover for my book because it's my mom's favorite picture of me. She said I was always going "exploring!" Little did I know how many adventures awaited me!

For my kids, Shelley and Ty, and my grandson, Cody.
May their lessons from God always be gentle ones.

CONTENTS

PREFACE

Several years ago, I began writing short stories about my childhood experiences for a Sunday devotional on my social media page. It was my intention to reveal how God uses our everyday experiences to "train us up." After many Sundays had passed, some members of my family and many of my friends began to encourage me to combine these stories into book form. After a while, I began to pray about it and ask God to guide me and help me with the decision. Well…. the result is this book, and it is my heartfelt prayer that God will use the stories to touch, heal, comfort, and encourage those who read them, and to draw them closer to Him.

In every situation in our lives, God has a lesson. We just need to look for it and learn from it. Lessons are learned every day, but sometimes we don't realize it until much later in life. Sometimes these lessons are gentle and sometimes they're harsh; but God's lessons are always intended to strengthen our relationship with Him. Sometimes we don't even *know* we learned anything… we just did. As I was writing these stories about my childhood, God made me aware that He was always at work in my life, and He was the most understanding and patient of Teachers. It is my hope and prayer, and the purpose of this book, that each of you can look back and see God's lessons in your life as well… and learn from them.

Thank you to my family members and many friends who encouraged me to compile my stories into a book, and to all those mentioned in my book… thank you for the memories!

Disclaimer: Many times, our memories aren't quite the same as the memories of the other person who was included in the same event. We all see and remember different versions of the same thing, and from a different perspective. So, if you are in one of my stories, and your memory is a little different from mine, so be it. I've written my stories just as I remember them happening, and I hope you enjoy them.

1

Bit the Baby

Some lessons learned are more painful than others. I don't have many memories of my early childhood, but there's one that stands out vividly because the images are indelibly printed in my mind. It involves a tiny baby, my daddy, and church.

When I was around four years old, I loved going into the baby nursery at church to look at the tiny little people in their cribs. My eyes were only about mattress level, but if I stood on my tiptoes, I could look see their faces and talk to them.

One Sunday morning, I was standing by one of the cribs, gazing at the sweetest little baby sound asleep, its arm hanging down between the slats. That little hand was so pudgy and soft, with dimples where knuckles should be. I don't know why in the world I did it, but I moved closer and placed that fat little hand inside my mouth....and bit down. The baby immediately let out a loud wail and continued to scream at the top of its lungs. My short legs couldn't carry me out of there fast enough! As I ran down the hallway, I looked up and saw my daddy coming toward me, followed closely by the nursery worker. She had seen me bite the baby, and as I stood there in shame, I heard her recount the incident to Daddy.

I couldn't deny it because, indeed, there were little red bite marks on the baby's hand. "Tarvah, did you bite that little baby's hand?" he asked me. With tears rolling down my cheeks, I slowly nodded. Daddy immediately squatted down on his toes, took my hand in his, and held it in one of his large hands. With the other hand, he softly stroked mine, as if petting a puppy. I looked into his eyes and started to feel better, since Daddy wasn't mad at me after all. He did that for a while without saying a word, and then he bent his head down over my hand. I began to smile, thinking he was going to kiss it. To my horror, he slowly opened his mouth and bit my hand. Suddenly, two wailing voices echoed throughout the church. It really hurt! He let me cry for a while before wrapping me in his arms and hugging me. When I finally stopped crying, he held me at arm's length and asked, "Did that hurt, Tarvah?" I nodded, unable to speak due to the lump in my throat. "Now you know how that little baby felt," he said. "You're really sorry you did that, aren't you?" I nodded again. "Are you ever going to bite anyone anymore?" he asked. This time I shook my head slowly from side to side, and with tears still on my face I managed to say, "I'm sorry,

Daddy. I won't do it again." Daddy stood up, picked me up in his arms, and kissed me on the cheek. "I love you, honey, and I didn't want to hurt you, but you needed to be punished for doing something wrong so you won't do it again. Everything is okay now." I'd done something bad, but Daddy still loved me. And I loved him. You can be sure that I never, ever bit anyone again!

I didn't realize it at the time, but that experience paved the way for me to understand how God can chastise me and still love me. His correction assures me of His love because, if He didn't love me, He wouldn't care enough to train me in His ways.

Hebrews 12:11 – "No discipline seems pleasant at the time, but painful. Later on, however, it produces a harvest of righteousness and peace for those who have been trained by it."

Hebrews 12:6 – "For the LORD disciplines those he loves, and he punishes each one he accepts as his child."

Revelation 3:19 – "As many as I love, I rebuke and chasten: be zealous therefore, and repent."

Me, about the time I bit the baby's hand

2
Mamaw and the Earthworms

"Why are you smashing that old banana, Mamaw?" I asked. I was almost five years old, and we were sitting at the kitchen table as I watched my grandmother mash an old banana in a bowl until it turned into banana mush. "I'm going to feed my worms, Tarvah. Want to watch me?" she replied. Feed her *worms*? Of course, I did! Who wouldn't want to see that? I was picturing a worm, opening its mouth, chomping down on banana soup. Hahaha!

Well, I followed Mamaw through the kitchen door to the gallery where she headed toward a large #2 washtub. The gallery is what we called the long, covered back porch that extended the length of the house. When we got to the washtub, Mamaw said, "Here's my worm farm!" I saw that the tub was filled to the top with dirt and compost, but I sure didn't see any worms. Mamaw knelt by the washtub, placed the bowl of mashed-up banana on the floor, and began poking her finger way down into the dirt. She did this several times until there were finger holes all around in the tub. I kept watching closely, hoping to see worms poke their heads out, but to my surprise, Mamaw picked up the bowl and began spooning banana mush down each hole. When she was finished, she lightly brushed dirt back over the top of each hole. "But Mamaw… I didn't get to see any worms come eat the banana stuff," I whined. "How do you know they'll eat it?" "Oh, they'll eat it all right, just like they eat other fruit and vegetables I feed them. I'll be able to tell by how fat they are when I dig them up. "Why are you raising a tub full of old ugly worms?" I asked. Then she sat me down and explained that she really loved to go fishing, and she wanted to be sure she always had a fine bunch of bait ready at hand. When she wanted to go fishing, she'd just step out on the gallery, dig up some of the fattest earthworms you'd ever see, and off she'd go with her bucket of bait. "If you look forward to doing something you like, you always prepare ahead of time, Tarvah. That way, you'll always be ready," she said.

Mamaw had a big Bible she read every day, and one of my memories of her is when she was sitting in her rocking chair with that Bible in her hands… a Bible that is now one of my most prized possessions. Mamaw didn't just prepare for her fishing trips… she also prepared for the greatest trip of all that she would make someday; the trip to see Jesus. Little did I know that within the year, she would be making that trip. I know she was ready!

2 Timothy 2:15 – "Study to shew thyself approved unto God, a workman that needeth not to be ashamed, rightly dividing the word of truth."

3

Imaginary Friend

I remember way back in the day, when I was about three years old, I had an imaginary friend who accompanied me everywhere. This friend never, ever left my side, and I could always talk and play with him. He never got mad at me, and when we played games, he would always let me win. When I was sick, he would lie down beside me to make me feel better, and when I was scared, he would hold my hand and tell me he would keep me safe. He was the perfect friend! One day, while I was sitting on the couch looking at a book, my mom came sat down beside me, causing me to cry. When she asked me what in the world was wrong, I told her she had just sat on my friend. He was just that real to me. But you know what… I can't remember his name.

That time in my life prepared me well for my life with Jesus. I can envision Him walking by my side everywhere I go, and I can talk to Him anytime and anywhere. He comforts me and takes away my fear, promising to protect me. I know that He will always love me, even though He won't always let me win my "little games!" He is my Lord, Savior, and true Friend. He's genuinely real. And, most importantly, I always remember His name—Jesus!

1 Corinthians 3:16 – "Do you not know that you are a temple of God and that the Spirit of God dwells in you?"

Joshua 1: 9 – "Have not I commanded thee? Be strong and of a good courage; be not afraid, neither be thou dismayed: for the Lord thy God is with thee whithersoever thou goest."

Me, with a not-so-imaginary friend

4
Writing on the Blinds

Ever since I can remember, I have loved the color red. So, it was no wonder I got in real trouble when I picked my brightest red crayon to write on the shiny, white Venetian blinds in my bedroom. Keep in mind, I was only an "innocent" 5-year-old girl at the time. (My step-grandmother was the first-grade teacher, and she had already taught me how to read and write.) I had discovered that when I opened the blinds, no one could see the writing and I was the only one who knew it was there. I forgot that those blinds would be closed at night and would remain that way until I woke up. Uh-oh.

Daddy happened by the room one morning before I got up, and the blinds were still closed. There they were—glaring red words on a shiny white background, staring right toward my bedroom door for all to see. Needless to say, I was disciplined for such behavior, and believe me, those words were a lot harder to remove than they were to put on! However, the punishment was tempered with love and a big hug afterward, because, you see, the words I had written on the blinds were, "I love Daddy."

I loved Daddy

Daddy was a deacon at First Baptist Magnolia, and as I think back on my childhood, I reflect on how he modeled the relationship I now have with my Heavenly Father. God disciplines us with love and compassion, but if we know Him personally through His Son, His arms are always there to hold us close, and He delights in hearing us tell Him that we love Him. Daddy went home to be with the Lord in 1969 when I was only 24. I still miss him a lot. He never failed to give me a hug and assure me that he still loved me after I'd been punished for something I'd done wrong.

Thanks, Daddy, for helping me to see how God will always love me too.

Proverbs 3:12 – "For the Lord corrects those he loves, just as a father corrects a child in whom he delights."

5
Goat Pills

Things aren't always what they seem. I learned this important lesson at the tender age of four, although I didn't realize it at the time. On this particular day, Auntie had gone with our family to visit Aunt Joyce and Uncle Ruel. I loved to visit them because they raised goats, and one of my favorite things to do was watch the baby goats jump around and play. After we had visited for a while, Auntie looked at me and asked, "Tarvah, do you want to go to the goat pen and see the babies?" Well, she didn't have to ask me twice, and I jumped up and down, grabbed her by the hand, and nearly dragged her to the door. We had to go through a pasture where the goats had freely roamed before we got to the pen.

As we were walking along, I happened to look down and see a whole bunch of tiny black balls in a heap on the ground. Jerking my hand away from Auntie, I ran over to them saying, "Pills, pills, pills… I never saw so many pills! Think I'll take a few!" Reaching down, I grabbed up as many as my chubby little hand could hold. Looking on in total horror, Auntie shouted, "Tarvah, stop! Throw those down!" I couldn't figure out why she was so upset, and I just stood there looking at her as she had this strange look on her face. "Those aren't pills," she told me, "That's where the little goats have gone to the bathroom!" Ugh!! I couldn't get those things out of my hand quick enough! As I opened my hand, there were a couple that didn't want to drop off and I shook my hand vigorously to get them to let go.

Needless to say, our trip to the goat pen was slightly delayed as we had to go back to the house and give my hand a thorough scrubbing. On the way back, Auntie patiently explained, "Tarvah, you'll learn that things aren't always what they look like, and you'll have to be careful to check them out before you do anything." Yep! She sure knew what she was talking about. And you can bet that I've never forgotten that lesson! (What also helped me remember was that it became a favorite family story that was retold time after time.)

Now, that was a silly little story, but it illustrates one of Jesus' greatest warnings in his Sermon on the Mount. Things, and people, aren't always what they seem, and we need to stay aware.

Matthew 7:15 – "Beware of false prophets, which come to you in sheep's clothing, but inwardly they are ravening wolves."

Me, about the time of the goat pills

6

The Quarter

I remember one time when I was about four years old, and I had a quarter. I felt like I was rich! I remember it just like it was yesterday, holding it tightly in my hand so I wouldn't lose it. To me, it was a huge sum of money, and I wasn't about to turn it loose. All the ice cream I could buy with that quarter! There was no way I was going to lose it! Then along came my nine-year-old brother, Jimmy. He had three nickels in his possession, and he knew an easy mark when he saw one. Taking me by the hand, he led me into my huge, walk-in closet and said to me, "How would you like to have three monies instead of just one?" Of course, that sounded great to me, and I quickly made the deal. Gosh, now I was truly rich!

What a great big brother I had! I could now buy cookies to go along with all that ice cream. What Jimmy didn't count on, was me running to Mom and telling

her what a great thing he had done for me. Needless to say, Jimmy got in a lot of trouble and he had to give my quarter back. I wasn't really sure that was such a good thing until Mom told me the quarter was really worth five nickels. I learned a valuable lesson that day, though. It's not the money that causes grief... it's the desire to always have more!

1 Timothy 6: 10 – "For the love of money is the root of all evil."

I was excited about those nickels

7

Percy

Cats are very strange creatures. I first discovered this at the tender age of five or six when I was introduced to Percy, Aunt Joyce's tomcat. Percy and I became great friends (or so I thought). He liked me to rub him between his ears, and he especially seemed to enjoy it when I scratched him on his back right at the base of his tail. He'd raise his tail and make his hind legs stiff, pushing against my fingers as he purred contentedly. I really liked to pick him up and snuggle him against my cheek. He was so soft and warm. I loved Percy, but it wasn't too long before I began to wonder if that emotion was shared. Sometimes when I'd hug him, he'd struggle to get away, and if I didn't turn loose quick enough, I'd receive a quick scratch. Then there were times when I'd call him and he'd just give me a distant look, blink his eyes sleepily, and turn around go his own way.

One day when I was visiting Aunt Joyce, I was particularly persistent in my attention to Percy, and he ran away from me. Like several homes in town, Aunt Joyce and Uncle Ruel had a windmill in their backyard, and when I went around the house looking for Percy, I heard a really loud meow. I looked up and saw him high up on the wooden windmill frame. "Don't worry, Percy, I'll help you," I told him. Up the windmill I climbed. Tarvah to the rescue! When I finally got up beside him, he just looked at me, and I swear it looked like he was smiling. He gave me a couple of quick blinks, and then back down the windmill he went. As my eyes followed him down, they also noticed how high off the ground I was. Immediately I hugged the windmill frame with all my might. I was too scared to breathe, much less move, and like all kids when they get in trouble, I yelled for help. "Aunt Joyce, Aunt Joyyyyce!" I hollered. I heard the screen door slam shut and then Aunt Joyce was at the foot of the windmill, calling up to me, "Tarvah, what are you doing up there?"

"I came up to get Percy," I wailed.

"You get down from there right now or you're going to fall and hurt yourself!"

Well… that was really what I needed to hear. She was just confirming my worst fear. "No!" I replied, "I'm scared!" The next sound I heard was the ladder being placed against the windmill, and up came Aunt Joyce to help me down. The mighty rescuer turned out to have to be rescued herself! As I reached the ground, that treacherous Percy had the gall to come rub himself against my legs, purring loudly as if he'd done nothing wrong. But I knew what he was thinking. He'd led me up there and then left me high and dry to fend for myself. Some friend *he* was! From that time on, believe me, when Percy wanted to be left alone, I left him alone.

Looking back at that incident, I'm reminded of how many times in my life I've needed help; whether it was from something I'd done intentionally or something I'd foolishly blundered into without thinking. Thankfully, my "Rescuer" is always with me. Thank you, Father, for your faithfulness!

Joshua 1:9 – "Have I not commanded you? Be strong and courageous. Do not be afraid; do not be discouraged, for the LORD your God will be with you wherever you go."

8

The Butterfly

While watching a beautiful swallowtail butterfly on my lantana one day, a flashback brought a frown to my face because the butterfly I was picturing in my mind wasn't quite so beautiful.

I was about five or six years old, and as always when I was a kid, I had been exploring outside. On the ground, under a large bush, I found a hard, funny-looking object that looked like a little mummy, and it was stuck on a twig. Of course, I picked it up and ran to show it to Jimmy. Jimmy was almost five years older than me, and he knew just about everything. I knew he could tell me what it was. "It's a pupa," he told me. "After a long time, it will turn into a butterfly." Well, I had thought Jimmy knew everything, but this time I figured he was just pulling my leg. Seeing the look on my face, he said, "Why don't you keep it, and you'll see for yourself?" That was a great idea!

First, I had to fix something to keep it in… something that I could see through. Running into the house, I found a large jar with a metal lid. This would be perfect! With an ice pick, I carefully punched several holes in the lid so the butterfly could breathe when it emerged from that shell thing. I also picked a bunch of green leaves and placed them in the jar, along with several other twigs. It became somewhat crowded in there, but in my little uneducated mind, there was plenty of stuff for the new butterfly to eat, and lots of places for it to rest on. I knew it would be tired and hungry when it finished becoming a butterfly.

After I completed my project, I placed the twig with the pupa on it down into the jar and took it up to my room so I could check it every day. After a couple of days, I noticed that nothing had changed, and I began to get suspicious that Jimmy was pulling a joke on me after all. When a week had passed, so had my interest, and I forgot all about the silly old thing. It sure hadn't turned out to be very exciting.

Then one day, I happened to glance over at the jar and noticed that something had happened. A beautiful butterfly was in the jar! It had happened just like Jimmy said it would. I watched in awe as it crawled around, but something seemed to be terribly wrong. Its wings weren't big and beautiful like they should be. They were just small and kinda crumpled. By putting all that stuff in the jar with the pupa, I had not given the butterfly enough room to fully spread its wings. I grabbed the jar and ran outside to turn it loose, thinking that maybe if I got it out of the jar and put it in an open area, the wings would spread out. I carefully placed it on the lower branch of a tree, but all it did was just crawl clumsily around with wings that were twisted and disfigured. I felt a large tear begin to roll down my cheek, and I turned and walked away. I just couldn't watch any more. Later in the day, I went back to check on the butterfly, but it was gone. I tried to make myself think it had miraculously fixed its wings and flown away, but in my heart I knew better. It was probably a noon-time meal in some hungry bird's stomach. Why hadn't I asked someone how to do this right instead of just doing it my way? I had really messed up. Not only did I learn a hard lesson for myself, but it had come at the cost of something that otherwise would have been beautiful and free.

Now I have learned that when I seek God's direction in the choices and decisions I make, and when I'm obedient to His will, things turn out quite a bit better than my experience with that poor butterfly from my youth.

James 1:5 – "If any of you lacks wisdom, you should ask God, who gives generously to all without finding fault, and it will be given to you."

Proverbs 3:5-6 – "Trust in the Lord with all thine heart and lean not unto thine own understanding. In all thy ways acknowledge Him, and He will direct thy paths."

Jimmy and me about the time of the butterfly incident. (This is the bike he later taught me to ride.)

9
Auntie and the Footprint

"In the Sweet By and By" was my great-great aunt Willie Mae Sanders' favorite song, and we sang it at her funeral. Auntie lived next door to us when I was growing up, and she was like a grandmother to me. She loved serving the Lord and took it upon herself to clean the Methodist church and the parsonage that housed the "young preacher boys" (as she called them) when they pastored the church.

I spent many Saturdays "helping" her at the church when I was five or six years old. It was my job to place the handheld fans in the pews so people could fan themselves when it got a little warm. It took me a long time to get them all placed just right because each one had a beautiful picture on it, and I had to look at all of them. My favorite was one of a huge angel hovering over two little children while they played.

Auntie loved me with all her heart, and she never seemed to get mad at me or scold me, just gave me "gentle" correction. One day, she had just finished painting the wood floor between her rugs with a glossy gray paint. When I walked in the door, she warned me to be careful and not step on the freshly painted floor. At this point, I need to tell you that I was always barefooted when I was a kid and had a bad habit of not retaining instructions. Sure enough, it wasn't long until I accidentally placed one of my bare feet right in the middle of a strip of floor she had just painted. I stood there staring in horror at the very clear evidence of my misdeed, and with paint all over the bottom of my foot, I hopped to the front door and took off for home next door as fast as I could go!

I decided to wait a few days before going back to Auntie's, hoping that the paint had dried, and my footprint would have somehow miraculously disappeared. Several days later, I got up the nerve to go back. The first thing I did when I got inside her house was to go check it out, and there it was, my footprint, painted bright red! Oh, it really stood out against that shiny, gray background! Auntie just laughed and looked at me with a twinkle in her eye, and never said a harsh word. I loved her so much for that.

What a wonderful Christian role model she was to me, and I'm so happy that we will have a wonderful reunion one day. "In the sweet, by and by… we will meet on that beautiful shore." Yes, Auntie modeled her love for her Lord by always loving me and forgiving me, usually accompanied by a huge hug!

Ephesians 4:3 – "Be kind to one another, tender-hearted, forgiving each other, just as God in Christ also has forgiven you."

10

Milking Aunt Ed's Cow

"Grip it with your whole hand, Tarvah, and pinch your thumb and first finger together at the top. Then slowly squeeze with your other fingers, one at a time." I heard Aunt Ed's instructions, but it wasn't quite that easy for my little five-year-old fingers. But then, I'm getting a little ahead of my story.

Back when I was growing up in Magnolia, there was no shortage of babysitters for my mom to choose from. My grandparents lived just down the street, Auntie lived next door, and Auntie's sister, Aunt Ed, lived just across the railroad tracks close to the Baptist Church. There is now a concrete parking lot where her house used to stand. Her name was actually Edith, but we all called her "Aunt Ed." I didn't stay with her too often, but when I did, it was fun. She had chickens, a dog, a cat with kittens, and best of all, a milk cow. Boy could Aunt Ed milk that cow! I loved watching her squirt that stream of milk into the bucket until it began to foam.

"Let me do it, Aunt Ed!" I begged one day. "Let me try. I can do it!" She finally smiled and, getting up from the stool, she began the lesson. "You have to sit close and lean your head against her stomach so she'll know you're there," she said, "and watch out for her tail. She'll switch you with it, and she might even try to kick you."

"I will, I will," I hurriedly told her as I sat on the stool. Then she told me how to grip the teat and explained what I had to do to get the milk to come out. I tried really hard, but nothing happened. Squeezing my eyes shut with the effort, I tried again. Nothing. Then I began jerking hard out of frustration, and that didn't work, for sure!

"Whoa," said Aunt Ed. "You're not going to get any milk that way. Take your hand away and start over. Slow down and do it just the way I told you. You have to squeeze your fingers in the right order, and you can't squeeze them all at the same time. Before long, you'll get some milk to come out, but you have to do it right. It just takes practice."

Placing my hand in the correct position, I began the sequence again. Pinch, squeeze, pull… pinch, squeeze pull. Gosh, this is really a lot harder than it looks. Every once in a while, that silly cow would turn her head and look back at me as if to say, "What in the world is that child trying to do?"

It was frustrating to milk the cow, and my hand was getting tired and beginning to cramp. Aunt Ed could see my discouragement, so she suggested I take a minute to rest as she explained the process again in great detail. Determined to succeed, I placed my hand in position for the third time and began to pinch and squeeze. For a couple of attempts, nothing happened. Then, there it was! A drop of milk fell out, followed by a couple of drops, and finally, a small stream. I did it! I was milking the cow! I looked around to see if Aunt Ed was watching. "Good job, Tarvah!" she said with a huge smile on her face. "See…it just took a little practice." Gosh, I was one happy little girl. Not only was I able to milk the cow, but I also made Aunt Ed proud of me!

That memory brings a smile to my face, but it also reminds me of an important lesson. Doing something the right way to get a good result needs practice. This principle applies to my Christian life too. Maybe if I practice enough, I'll get it right and bring a smile to God's face. I would like that.

This chorus from the hymn, "Our Best" sums it up perfectly. "Every work for Jesus will be blest. But He asks from everyone his best. Our talents may be few… these may be small. But unto Him is due, our best, our all."

Colossians 3:23 – "Whatever you do, work at it with all your heart, as working for the Lord, not for human masters."

Milking a cow is hard for a five-year-old!

11
Servel and Hardwick

It wasn't "cat" or "dog" that I learned how to spell first; it was "Servel" and "Hardwick". You see, when I was five or six years old, I spent a lot of time next door at Auntie's house, and Auntie spent a lot of time in her kitchen. In that kitchen, she had a Servel icebox and a Hardwick stove. It was a gas refrigerator, but we still called it an icebox back then. Auntie, a retired schoolteacher before becoming a postmistress, loved to teach a little five-year-old girl how to spell. "What's the name of my icebox, Tarvah?" she'd ask, while rolling out cookie dough. "How do you spell it?" Then she'd do the same for the stove. "Look at the word, Tarvah. Close your eyes and see the letters," she'd say as she popped the cookies into the oven. Auntie loved to teach and cook. It seemed she was always in the kitchen, and she always had a happy face while she was there. But then, she almost always had a happy face everywhere she went.

We didn't have air conditioning back then, so during the summer, everyone's windows were open, and I could always tell when Auntie was in the kitchen because such good smells would float through the air to our house. What could a kid do but run and check them out? Teacakes or pies baking, black-eyed peas and cornbread, fried chicken—everything that made a kid feel happy and warm and cozy inside. When she made pie crust, she'd make extra dough and let me slice little strips and sprinkle cinnamon and sugar on them to bake with the pies. They were so crispy and good right out of the oven. *Mmmm.*

Auntie made learning fun because her kitchen was a happy place, and I learned a lot of good stuff there. When I was older, she loved to help me memorize Bible verses too. She'd start with short verses. "Read the verse, close your eyes, and see the words." Auntie loved the Lord with all her heart, and I considered her one of the saints. Over the years, I have committed many scripture verses to memory, and it's funny; I have always closed my eyes while doing it. It's pretty amazing how those scriptures pop into my mind whenever I need them. "Close your eyes, Tarvah… see the words."

Deuteronomy 6:6-7 – "And these words, which I command thee this day, shall be in thine heart. And thou shalt teach them diligently unto thy children, and shalt talk of them when thou sittest in thine house, and when thou walkest by the way, and when thou liest down, and when thou risest up."

12

Auntie's Fried Chicken

Fried chicken. The words alone can excite your taste buds. It's one of my favorite dishes, but nobody made it quite like my great-great aunt, Willie May Sanders, whom we called Auntie. If you've been reading my posts, you will recall that she lived next door to us when I was growing up. If the smell of that chicken frying wafted over to our house, I'd be at her door in a heartbeat. However, my first experience with the preparation of fried chicken wasn't quite so appetizing.

When I was around six years old, my dad was called back into service for the Korean War and had to report to San Diego. My mom went with him to see him off, but since I had already started first grade, I stayed in Magnolia with Auntie. Auntie kept a few chickens that she would pen up at night, and she also had a spunky little dog named Big'Un that I loved to play with.

One morning, Auntie and I were feeding the chickens outside, and she asked me if I wanted fried chicken for lunch. Naturally, I said yes, but I wasn't prepared for what happened next. To my horror, she bent down and grabbed one of her hens by the neck. The hen started squawking as Auntie lifted it up and began whipping it around in the air, wringing its neck. She dropped it back to the ground and blood went everywhere. The chicken flopped right towards me, where I was standing with my mouth open, and I started to run away, yelling as Big'Un barked, and Auntie laughed. Looking back, it must have been a comical sight, but at the time, I was not amused.

After the chicken drew its last breath, Auntie chopped off its head and left it on the back steps while she boiled a huge pot of water. Once the water was ready, she dunked the chicken in it and began plucking off the feathers. If you've never smelled hot, wet chicken feathers, you just haven't lived yet. Auntie then cleaned and gutted the chicken before cutting it up into pieces and preparing it for frying. Through all of this, I just stood there, watching in a mix of shock and fascination as she completed the preparations for my fried chicken dinner.

You'd think that witnessing that gory process, I'd have lost my appetite for fried chicken, but that wasn't the case. It smelled so good while cooking, looked so nice and crisp on the platter, and tasted even better as I crunched into it. I still love fried chicken to this day!

Auntie always had a surprise waiting for me whenever I visited her. She would give the best bear hugs and was always so happy to see me. Whether it was cookies, a special story, or something she had made for me, I always looked forward to going to Auntie's house to see what she had for me. She once even made me a little sun bonnet that looked just like hers.

Thinking about Auntie, I can't help but wonder what will be waiting for me when I see Jesus.

1 Corinthians 2:9 – "But as it is written: 'Eye has not seen, nor ear heard, nor have entered into the heart of man the things which God has prepared for those who love Him.'"

Me with Auntie and her dog, Lassie

13

Daddy's Cigarette Lighter

Sometimes it's the silliest things that can make a person scream. When I was six years old, I heard my mom do this very thing at the sight of an ordinary item. But let me start at the beginning of the story.

My dad served in the Navy during the Korean War, and we hadn't seen him in a long time. The only communication my mom had with him was through his letters. One day, she received a special letter from Daddy in the mail. Finally, the war had ended, and he would be coming home! He told her that when he was discharged in California, he would pick up his car on the naval base and head for Magnolia as fast as he could. Of course, we were all very excited and couldn't wait to see him again.

The days passed, and Mom checked the mail every day for a letter that would let us know that Daddy was on his way. Sure enough, before too long, a letter came saying that he was in California and would be home soon. We began to count the days, and count the days, and count some more. No letter, no phone call, just the passing of days… and endless questions. "When is Daddy coming home?" "Is Daddy gonna be here tomorrow?" "How much longer, Mom?" Then one afternoon, my mom picked me up from school and we headed home. Jimmy hadn't gotten home yet, so it was just the two of us. Mom opened the front door and we stepped into the entrance hall, and that was when it happened. She let out a shrill scream that literally froze me in my tracks. I was so scared I couldn't move, but at the same time, I was trying to figure out what had made her scream. "Dub!" she shouted. Then I saw it. There was Daddy's cigarette lighter just sitting there by itself on the back of a chair. She had screamed at a cigarette lighter! Daddy was home! But where was he? I went running ahead of her to look for him, running all through the house as I heard her doing the same thing. As I passed the closet door in the back bedroom, I noticed that it was open just a little bit. Running over to it, I threw the door open and there was Daddy!

I can still see that image today. He was dressed in his navy uniform and was squatting down with his finger over his lips, wanting me to be quiet and not give him away. What? How could I be quiet when my Daddy was home? As he reached out and grabbed me in his arms, it didn't matter anyway because Mom was right behind me. He stood up with me in his arms and began to hug and kiss my mom. Oh, how wonderful it all was! "Dub, why didn't you call me at work when you got here," my mom asked him. "Because I wanted to surprise you," he told her. As it turned out, he had left the car down the street at Papaw's house so we wouldn't see it and walked home from there. Oh, he surprised her alright. That's the first time I ever realized that people sometimes cry when they're happy. Wow! Daddy was home!

That memory makes me think about the time Jesus will return to this earth, and how much I eagerly anticipate His coming. He's left signs already, but when will He come? Is He coming soon? Will He be here tomorrow? I can hardly wait to see Him!

Mark 13:32-33 – "But about that day or hour no one knows, not even the angels in heaven, nor the Son, but only the Father. Be on guard! Be alert! You do not know when that time will come."

Revelation 22:20 – "He which testifieth these things saith, Surely, I come quickly. Amen. Even so, come, Lord Jesus."

Daddy was home

14
Auntie's Washing Machine

One day, when I was about five or six years old, I was "helping" Auntie wash her clothes. Auntie's washing machine was a large metal tub with a detachable wringer, and she used a metal scrub board to scrub the clothes with. The wringer consisted of two parallel wooden rollers, a hand crank, and a long metal arm that you could attach to the tub. Auntie would fill the tub with soapy water, and then individually scrubbed each piece of laundry by rubbing it on the scrub board. When she finished scrubbing, she would drain the tub and fill it with clean water several times in order to completely rinse the clothes. Then came my favorite part. Auntie would attach the wringer to squeeze all the water out of the clothes before taking them outside to hang on the clothesline. With one hand she would feed the piece of laundry into the wringer, while with the other hand she would turn the crank. A lump of soggy wet material would enter the rollers on one side, and when it came out on the other side it looked like a flat piece of cardboard. It was amazing!

Well, one washday I told Auntie that I wanted to help, and the first thing she had me do was wash one of my shirts. Placing the scrub board into the wash tub, I quickly picked up my shirt, dunked it a couple of times into the soapy water, and began to scrub it on the metal scrub board. Now if you've never washed clothes on a scrub board, you have no idea how complicated and dangerous it can be. As I began to rub my shirt up and down across the ribbed metal, I scraped one of my knuckles. "Ouch, that hurt!" I shouted, dropping the shirt down into the water. "Go ahead and finish it, Tarvah," Auntie told me. "You'll learn to be more careful." I picked up the shirt and began gingerly moving it across the board. "You have to scrub harder if you want to get it clean," Auntie told me. Now I didn't really care if it got clean or not, but I was already committed to washing the thing, so I scrubbed just a little bit harder.

I finally finished the shirt, managing to only whack one more knuckle in the process, and decided I'd had enough of the washing part. "Okay, Auntie. I've finished my shirt. Now you can do the rest and I'll help with the wringer part,"

I told her. I was really looking forward to doing that wringer thing! So, Auntie smiled patiently and finished the washing. Then finally it was time for the wringer! "I'll turn the crank while you feed the clothes into it," I told Auntie eagerly. She just smiled, picked up a pair of pants, and began feeding them into the rollers. I grabbed the crank with one hand and began to turn it. Then I had to use both hands. This was harder than I thought. This wasn't fun. "I know. I'll feed the clothes into the wringer while you crank," I told Auntie. Again, she just smiled as we changed places, and she cautioned me to be careful putting the clothes between the rollers. I picked up a shirt and carefully began feeding it into the wringer. Auntie turned the crank and the shirt came out the other side, flat as a pancake. This was fun! Then I picked up a sock. Socks are short. As I held it up to the roller, I began watching to see how it would look when it came out the other side. Did I mention that socks are short? I got so engrossed at how it was looking when it came through the rollers that I didn't turn loose in time and my finger went into the wringer. "Owwww!" I hollered. I tried to pull my finger out but it was stuck tight! Jumping up and down just made it hurt worse! Quickly Auntie backed the crank up, and when my finger came loose, she wrapped her arms around me as I sobbed. I was scared to look at my finger because I thought it would look like that flat sock! Before too long the hurt eased off and, to my great relief, my finger wasn't flat at all, just a little red on the end. This clothes-washing business sure wasn't as much fun as I thought it was!

As a final note, today, as I loaded the machine that does all the washing for me, I thought about how richly God has blessed me, and how I take His blessings for granted. Even in my unworthiness, He provides for my every need. To Him be all glory and praise.

Philippians 4:19 – "And this same God who takes care of me will supply all your needs from his glorious riches, which have been given to us in Christ Jesus."

15

The Snuff Can

I wonder what it is about telling kids not to do something, that makes them go ahead and do it anyway? Curiosity? Hard-headedness? Stubbornness? Probably a combination of all three. When I was about five or six years old, my parents hired a lady to come take care of Jimmy and me while they worked. I remember Mary Mayes was very patient and tolerant with me, and I always had fun when she was there. One afternoon, Mary was sitting outside under the oak trees shelling peas. I loved to watch her do that. She could make those peas pop out of their shells quicker than you could say, "Jack Spratt!" Anyway, one day while she was busy with the peas, she looked up at me and asked me to do something for her. "Tarvah…will you please run inside and get my can of snuff?" she asked. Then she said something that she shouldn't have said. "Be sure you don't open the lid." What? Don't open the lid? Why not? Off I went into the house to find her snuff. Our house was built up off the ground on building blocks, and we had to go up four concrete steps to a small porch at our back door. I didn't have any problem finding her can of snuff, but on the way back outside I kept hearing the words in my mind, "Don't open the lid." I fought the temptation for a little while, but I just HAD to see what was inside. As I got to the back door, my little fingers began prying on the lid. Finally, "pop," off came the lid about the same time I tripped on the top step. Down I went, tumbling all the way to the ground, engulfed in a large brown cloud. Snuff went everywhere! Up my nose, in my eyes, and in my mouth. I couldn't see, I couldn't breathe, and I just knew I was going to choke to death. I could hear Mary laughing as she quickly came to my rescue, but then she stopped when she saw my distress. She immediately grabbed me up, took me into the kitchen, and began washing my face and telling me to blow my nose. After she finally got me cleaned up, she gave me a big hug and said, "I told you not to open that lid, Tarvah. When will you ever learn to mind?"

I find a huge parallel between my childish disobedience and our country's problems today. We have disobeyed God's commandments and ignored His warnings. We have turned our backs on His laws and continue to pay the consequences. I can just hear God saying, "When will you ever learn to mind? If you do, I will make you a promise." Oh, how I pray that we will finally learn to mind.

Jeremiah 7:28 – "Therefore say to them, 'This is the nation that has not obeyed the Lord it's God or responded to correction. Truth has perished; it has vanished from their lips.'"

2 Chronicles 7:14 – "If my people, which are called by my name, shall humble themselves, and pray, and seek my face, and turn from their wicked ways; then will I hear from heaven, and will forgive their sin, and will heal their land."

16

A Permanent from Bertie

"Oh, wow! I'm only six years old and I'm going to be in a wedding!" That was the thought that went through my head when I heard the news. My babysitter, Eloise Brantley, was going to get married and she wanted me to be her flower girl! Now I didn't know much about weddings, or flower girls, or stuff like that, but it sure sounded like fun to me. Little did I know how much preparation it took to get ready for a wedding.

The first inkling of "trouble" began when Mom called me in from playing and said we had to go to "Miss Catherine's" to let her fit me for my dress. Miss Catherine Damuth lived just across the railroad tracks, close to the Baptist Church, and she was a seamstress for our family and for almost everyone in Magnolia. Grudgingly, I went inside and got cleaned up. When we got to Miss Catherine's, I had to stand real still while she pinned a pattern on me and began to take measurements. This was just the first of many fittings that I had to stand still for, but finally my dress was finished, and I'll have to admit it was very pretty. I sure was glad to get all that over with! Little did I know that the worst was yet to come.

The day before the wedding, my mom told me I had an appointment at Bertie's to get a permanent. Bertie was Eloise's mother, and she owned the local beauty shop. Like Miss Catherine, she took care of almost everyone in Magnolia. Get a permanent? What? I couldn't go in my pigtails? Well, just knowing that I had to do this was bad enough, but when I walked into Bertie's and saw "the machine," I froze in my tracks. There stood this thing that I can only describe as a huge mushroom with tentacles hanging down from it, and each tentacle had metal clips or rings hanging on the ends. And it was electric. I didn't like this at all. Not one little bit. "Mom, is Bertie going to hook me up to that machine," I asked. "Of course, Tarvah. How do you think your hair is going to get curled?" My mom answered. Slowly, I made my way to over to the thing and sat down, closing my eyes tightly. "Will it take long?" I asked Bertie, "And will it hurt?" "Of course, it won't hurt Tarvah, and you're going to be very pretty when we get through," she said. I noticed that she didn't say anything about how long it would take though.

Gathering up some strands of my long hair, she began the process of curling it around the little metal things. After what seemed like an eternity, she told me she was going to turn on the machine and the heat from the metal thingies would make my hair curl. Again, I squeezed my eyes tightly shut and held my breath. What if that electricity went through those clips and I got shocked? What if they got too hot and my hair caught on fire? I smelled something funny and got really scared, thinking my hair was being scorched, but Bertie said it was just the solution she put on my hair. Finally, she turned off the machine and removed the clips from my hair. Ahh, we were done! Then, as I started to get out of the chair, she said something awful! "Don't get up, Tarvah, we have to finish the rest of your hair." What? Go through all that again? It seems that I had too much hair to get it all done in one sitting, so now she had to do the other half! Good grief! And to think I was excited about being in this dumb wedding!

After another agonizing period of time, we were finally finished. I'll have to admit, my hair looked real pretty, and Mom and Bertie were just beaming! The next day we all got dressed for the big event, and when I saw myself in the mirror, I was pretty proud of myself. I looked just like a little princess!

Wow! I guess all the agony I went through was really worth it!

The memory of this time in my life reminds me of how God uses trials and hardships in our lives to grow us into the followers He wants us to be. As we trust in Him to carry us through, and then rediscover how faithful He is to do it, we not only become more beautiful in His sight, but we also realize that with Him, we have all that we need.

1 Peter 5:10 – "And after you have suffered a little while, the God of all grace, who has called you to his eternal glory in Christ, will himself restore, confirm, strengthen, and establish you."

Jimmy, Mom, Daddy, and me
on the big day of the wedding

Happy to be in the wedding!

17

The Devil's Helper

I decided I'd just be the devil's helper. Yep, if I was bad enough, he'd just make me a helper and then when I died I wouldn't have to be punished for the bad things I'd done. I'd just follow him around and do whatever he said and then he'd like me too much to punish me.

I can clearly remember when that thought raced through my mind. I was about five or six years old, sitting on the front steps of our house, and had just been punished for something that I can't even remember now. But it must have been bad because as I sat there, I began to think about the sermon from the previous Sunday; a sermon that we don't hear too often these days. It was about hell, and damnation, and eternal punishment for the evil that we do if we don't repent. At that time, I wasn't feeling very repentant though, just sitting there sulking and resentful for being punished. If I could just become the devil's friend, then he wouldn't do bad things to me. That thought then led to another. If I became his helper, then that meant that I would have to help him punish people. I didn't think I'd like that. I would also tempt people to hurt other people; sometimes even people they love. I sure wouldn't like to do that! Wouldn't it be more fun to become Jesus' helper and maybe become an angel? If I was Jesus' friend, every day would be happy. If I followed Him around and helped Him, then when I died, I'd become an angel. That way I could hug all the people that came to Heaven. I think I'd like that!

When I look back at that time, I realize it was pretty silly to think like that. But that's how little kids think sometimes. It might not have been theologically sound, but I believe it was at that point that I began to think about how to live my life. It took me four more years to make my decision to become a follower of Jesus Christ, but I can point to that tender age of five or six as the time when I began to think of eternity, and where I would spend it.

One of the songs we sang in church one morning triggered that old memory, and I love to sing it. "Take up thy cross and follow me, I heard my Master say. I gave my life to ransom thee. Surrender your all today."

John 3:16 – "For God so loved the world, that he gave his only begotten Son, that whosoever believeth in him should not perish, but have everlasting life."

18

Pork Chop Bones

I love pork chops. Can't remember a time when I didn't. I really like to chew the meat off the bone, and when it's just family around I still do that. One day when we had pork chops for lunch, I picked up the bone to do my favorite thing and it brought back a not-so-pleasant memory.

My parents were good friends with Howard and Inez Davenport, and we spent a lot of time visiting at their house. Daddy and Howard would play their guitars and we would all have a great time sitting around singing. One evening, when I was about four or five years old, we went to see them right after supper. Since everyone was eager to begin the jam session, Inez said she would just leave their supper dishes on the table and clean them up later. I really liked to sit and listen to them sing and would happily join in when I knew the songs. Sometimes Jimmy liked to sing along too, but he usually had his comic books with him and would just read them when he got bored.

After we had been singing a while, I got thirsty and wandered into the kitchen to get a drink of water. Passing by the dining room table, I happened to notice that Inez had fried pork chops for supper and in each plate, there were several bones with meat left on them. Wow, this was a great find! Piling all the bones onto one plate, I looked around for a place to hide and enjoy my treasure. Even at that tender age, I somehow knew that Mom would not be happy about me doing this. The tablecloth hung about halfway to the floor, so thinking that it would be a great place to hide, I crawled under the table and proceeded to chew the meat off those bones. Gosh, Inez sure could cook pork chops!

I was just about through gnawing on all the bones when I saw my mom's feet approaching and heard her call out, "Tarvah, where are you?" Oh, no! Scrunching my feet up closer to me, I sat real still, hoping she wouldn't see me. Evidently, I wasn't hidden as well as I thought because the next thing I knew, she was raising up the tablecloth and I was busted! Peeping at me under the table, with her head turned sideways, she said, "What on earth are you doing under there?" Well, it was plenty plain to see what I was doing. I had a plate of pork chop bones in my lap, a bone in my hand, and probably pork chop "residue" all over my face. To make it all even worse, Inez came walking up right behind her and she saw me too. Of course, my mom was mortified! Here sat her little girl, hiding under a table, gnawing on bones like a little starving child that hadn't eaten in days. Inez just burst out laughing, and soon my mom had joined in too. I guess it all was kinda funny, but at the time I just wanted to run away from them and hide again.

I got in a lot of trouble for that. Not just for chewing on the bones, but mostly for being sneaky and trying to hide while I was doing something I knew was wrong. Mom told me later that it was a good thing she and Inez were such good friends because she knew Mom hadn't been starving me! The incident became one of Inez's favorite stories, and fifty years later she still thought it was funny. Sometimes when she would see me somewhere she would even say with a laugh, "Tarvah, we're having pork chops for supper. Want me to save you some?"

As I grew older, I learned that I couldn't hide much from my mom, but I also learned an even more valuable lesson. There's absolutely nothing that I can hide from God.

Hebrews 4:13 – "Nothing in all creation is hidden from God's sight. Everything is uncovered and laid bare before the eyes of Him to whom we must give account."

I really loved to gnaw on those pork chop bones!

The Bathroom Confessional

I've always had a very active conscience. I must have been born with it. Ever since I was four or five years old, whenever I did something wrong, it would weigh heavy on me until I would feel sick. Mom would always know when something was wrong with me because I was never good at hiding my feelings. (I still can't do that.) The only thing that would help was "confessing" to my mom, and the bathroom was my confessional! When I couldn't stand it anymore, I'd go to my mom and say, "Mom, meet me in the bathroom." There, I would sit on the toilet seat, and she would sit on the edge of the bathtub, and I'd "come clean!" I'll never forget the feeling each time, as I'd say, "Do you still love me?" and she would hug and forgive me. It was like a huge weight was lifted off my chest. I'd done wrong, and she'd forgiven and loved me anyway. This is not to say that I never got punished, but the punishment was only temporary—her love was forever.

As I grew older, these experiences with Mom made it easy for me to understand God's love for me in the same way. She never went around quoting scriptures, nor pushing her own love for God on me, but she lived it in front of me, modeling God's love with her own actions. It was easy for me to transition

from my childhood experiences with her to my salvation experience with God. Confess my sins, be forgiven, and be loved forever. I'm so thankful she made sure that we will always be together for all eternity. Thank you, Mom, for not pushing and preaching, but *leading* me to know the Lord.

Isaiah 66:13 – "As a mother comforts her child, so I will comfort you…"

My mom loved me even when I did wrong

20

Jimmy—My Hero

I remember the day my big brother became my hero. It was a very special time in church one Sunday when I was about 5 years old, and Jimmy was about 10. Back then, there was no such thing as Children's Church, and kids always attended the regular service. Most of the time I didn't listen to what the preacher was saying, but when he preached about the Holy Ghost, or talked about the blood of Jesus, I sat up and paid attention.

On this particular Sunday, we had gone to the Methodist Church with Auntie, and Jimmy participated in his first Communion. I watched him as he made his way to the front of the church, and when he drank from the cup, I raised my face in awe and said to Auntie, "Auntie, did you see Jimmy? He drank that blood and stuff just like a little man!" That was just the beginning, and I started watching everything he did. As I grew older, I learned that he could throw a mighty mean fast ball. When I was about eight, I was catching him in the back yard and misjudged the pitch. Thank goodness it hit the web of my glove just before it hit me in the mouth, resulting in a bloody lip. He told me to be tough, so I learned to be tough. He showed me how to hold the ball and I tried hard to imitate the way he threw it. I practiced a lot until it just became natural. Sometimes he'd let me tag along when he went fishing, but I always had to catch my own grasshopper and bait my own hook. He showed me one time, then I was on my own, but I practiced doing it the way he showed me, and I got good at it. Once he let me try to cast with his new fly rod. He showed me how to do it, and then he laughed at my feeble efforts. I got better at it though, because I practiced hard, imitating just the way he did it. When he was about 12, he got a new red bike and he said I could ride it, but it was way too big for me. I couldn't get on it, and I couldn't reach the pedals. He showed me how to put it beside our porch and straddle the bike, and then push off. I got to where I did that pretty good. I discovered that if I pushed down hard enough on one pedal, the other pedal would come up so I could reach it with my other foot. He just grinned when he saw what I was doing. When I made the basketball team in high school, I even talked the coach, Mr. Hinton, into letting me wear #11 because that was Jimmy's number on his high school team. I worked hard to be able play as good as he did and practiced a lot until the drills felt natural. Of course, now I know Jimmy didn't actually drink real blood that long ago Sunday morning, but you know what? He's still my hero.

I can clearly see a parallel here with my spiritual life. God sent Jesus into this world not only to bring us all salvation, but to set the example for how we are to live our lives. I want to be like Him, so I just need to practice, practice until it becomes natural. I hope one day I'll get good at it.

Ephesians 5:1 – "Imitate God, therefore, in everything you do, because you are his dear children."

21

Tru-boy

I love dogs. Through the years, I've had lots of dogs and deeply loved them all, but there's one in particular that I learned to love the hard way.

Papaw had a big hunting dog named Tru-boy that he kept on a chain in his back yard. I don't remember what type of hunter he was, but what I do remember is that he was huge. At least he looked that way in the eyes of a very small four-year-old girl. "Tarvah, don't get too close to Tru-boy," Papaw used to tell me, "Because he might hurt you." Now I knew he wouldn't ever hurt me because he was my friend. Papaw just didn't understand. I loved to throw Tru-boy scraps of food and just sit there and talk to him, but I was always careful to stay just beyond the length of his chain. Well, almost always.

One day he was asleep on the other side of his doghouse, and I got a little too close before I called to him. When he looked up and saw that I had a treat for him, he bounded up and ran to me so fast that he knocked me down. Planting his two gigantic front paws in the middle of my chest, Tru-boy pinned me to the ground and reached for his treat. When I looked up into those huge, drooling, gaping jaws that were coming right at my face I let out a scream that could have been heard all the way down to Gene Adams' garage. As I lay there crying in fear, waiting for his jaws to clamp down on my little body, I suddenly felt a large wet tongue licking all over my face. Tru-boy loved me! The tears kept coming though because he still wouldn't let me get up and I was getting mad. About that same time Papaw came out of the house shouting at Tru-boy to get away. Running over to where we were, he pushed him off me and picked me up. Nothing felt better than having Papaw's arms around me as he carried me safely out of Tru-boy's reach. When he started to put me down, I just wrapped my arms around his neck and hung on as he gave me a big bear hug. From that day on I was always careful to stay out of Tru-boy's reach until he would calm down enough to let me pet him. As I grew older, we became great friends and companions, and I always felt safe when Tru-boy was around.

When I think about that very frightening time in my life, even though I remember the fear, my strongest memory is the feeling of safety in Papaw's strong arms. It brings to mind another of my favorite hymns.

> "Leaning, leaning... safe and secure from all alarms.
> Leaning, leaning... leaning on the everlasting arms"

Deuteronomy 33:27 – "The eternal God is a dwelling place, and underneath are the everlasting arms..."

22

Auntie's Peas and Hushpuppies

It's funny how sometimes the strangest things trigger a memory. We were eating black-eyed peas and cornbread one night for supper, and a picture image just popped into my mind.

I was about 6 years old, sitting at Auntie's dining room table eating fresh black-eyed peas and fried hushpuppies. It must have been lunch time, because the sun was shining in through her dining room windows, and I could hear the birds singing outside. With the windows open, there was a light breeze blowing in and I could smell the flowers that were blooming in her yard. It's weird that I can remember those things in such detail, but I guess it's because it was such a happy time in my life. I even remember telling Auntie how good they were!

Auntie had a special way of fixing those hushpuppies, and that's another picture image that I brought up from my library of memories. Auntie is standing at her kitchen counter with a small bowl of cornmeal in front of her, and a tea kettle of boiling hot water beside the bowl. She pours some of the boiling water into the cornmeal and runs her hands under the cold water flowing from her faucet. Then she quickly picks up a small amount of the real hot cornmeal mixture, pats it back and forth in her palms to flatten it out and drops it into the sizzling grease in her iron skillet. I'm asking her, "Auntie, why do you need the water so hot?" and she's answering me, "So the cornmeal will stick together, Tarvah. This way you don't need to use eggs." She repeats this process until we have a plate full of flat hushpuppies about four inches long and about ½ inch thick. They're just thick enough so that you can slice them in half and put lots of butter in them. Then I would crunch them up on my plate, pour the peas on top, and dig in! Auntie's fried chicken was my very favorite, but those peas and hushpuppies ran a close second! As I thought about my times with Auntie, another image came to mind. She's sitting on her couch reading her Bible. She did that, without fail, every day.

As I thought about those wonderful memories, I realized that I was smiling. And I had a warm feeling inside. And I was happy. Then I thought about the most important picture image in my mind… me, at the age of nine, holding Brother Gerald's hand and asking Jesus into my heart. I was smiling. And I had a warm feeling inside. And I was happy. And it is well with my soul.

Philippians 4:8 – "Finally, brothers, whatever is true, whatever is honorable, whatever is just, whatever is pure, whatever is lovely, whatever is commendable, if there is any excellence, if there is anything worthy of praise, think about these things."

23

The Yo-yo

I've always had a hard time taking "No" for an answer. I remember one time when I was about six years old, and Toby Smith had a small grocery store across the back alley from our house. In a rack in the toy area, sat a beautiful, green yo-yo that I just had to have, and it only cost fifteen cents. For some reason, my mom told me I couldn't have it, but I just couldn't get that yo-yo off my mind.

One day, I was over in the store looking at that yo-yo, and I saw that Toby had his onions on sale. I remembered that Papaw loved onions, so I got this neat idea. I charged ten cents worth of onions to our account, walked to Papaw's house with the onions, and sold them to him for a quarter. Back to the store I went, as fast as my little legs would go, paid off the onions and, had fifteen cents left over! That wonderful, green yo-yo was all mine!

When I got back home, I took it upstairs to my room and made sure no one saw it but me. I would have gotten away with it, but Papaw had just showed up at our house with the sack of onions, and told my parents the "cute" story. I remember coming in the house from playing outside, and Papaw was there. Something else was there too—that sack of onions sitting on the bookshelf. Once I saw that sack of onions sitting there, I knew I was in trouble! Quickly turning around, I headed for the bathroom and said, "Mom, come here a minute. I need to talk to you." (The bathroom was always my confessional!) But I didn't made it to the bathroom because I had to first get by my dad, and he was too quick for me. "Wait just a minute, young lady. You have some explaining to do," he said as he caught me by the arm. And so, the whole story came out. I had to take the yo-yo back to the store, get my money back from a grinning Toby, and give Papaw the fifteen cents extra that I had charged him for the onions. Toby thought it was a hoot that I had come up with such an idea, but my mom said I had a lesson to learn. Not only had I cheated my own grandfather, but I had to understand that "No" means "*No!*"

I have since discovered that many times God says "No" to my requests, and over time, it always turns out to be for my benefit. Several years ago, I prayed that we would be able to buy a certain house. The circumstances were never right, and I became angry and upset. When the fires came to Magnolia, that house was totally consumed. What a mess my family would have been in if we had bought that house! I wonder when I will stop questioning God and learn to totally trust Him when He tells me "No." I'm trying really hard.

Proverbs 3:5 – "Trust in the Lord with all thine heart; and lean not unto thine own understanding."

24

Dr. Coker

No kid likes to go to the doctor, and I was no exception. But I do remember a time when I was glad that one had come to see me. When I was in second grade, my parents had gone to California for a few weeks for Naval training for my dad. Jimmy and I were already enrolled in school, so we stayed behind. Jimmy stayed with Mamaw and Papaw, and I stayed with Auntie. I loved staying with Auntie. She cooked my favorite foods, and every day we had "reading time." I would snuggle up next to her on the couch while she read stories to me about Uncle Wiggily, Billy Whiskers, Reddy Fox, Sammy Jay, and Uncle Billy Possum. Those critters became some of my dearest friends during my early childhood.

One afternoon, I began to feel sick to my stomach and didn't want to hear any stories. Auntie always kept some Baby Percy on hand, so she gave me a couple of doses and put me to bed. For those of you who don't know about Baby Percy, (Baby Percy was a "back in the day" medicine, kinda like Pepto Bismol), it usually did the trick. But this time, it didn't work. Pretty soon, that Baby Percy came right back up and out... all over the bed and all over me! Patiently, Auntie changed the sheets and cleaned me up, and the next thing I knew, she was on the phone. Picking up the hand-held receiver, she gave the phone one long crank, and I heard her ask the operator to connect her with Dr. Coker's office in Tomball. *Oh, no! Not the doctor! I don't want a shot!* Just thinking about him coming with his needles made me sick all over again. I heard her telling the doctor my symptoms, and then she hung up and told me he was on his way.

Not too long after that, I heard a knock on the front door, and in came Dr. Coker. Dr. Coker wasn't a big man, but to me at that time, he looked huge. He had on black pants and a black coat, and even a black hat on top of a very thick head of white hair. But the thing I was concerned about was that *big black bag full of needles!* Coming over to the side of the bed, he leaned over me and said, "Now, what's wrong with you, young lady?" I just stared at him. Without waiting another second, he promptly stuck a thermometer in my mouth and then took his stethoscope out of the bag and began listening to my heart. After the examination was over, he told Auntie that I had the stomach virus that was going around, with a little touch of fever. He gave her a bottle of medicine and some baby aspirin (they actually carried that stuff with them back then) and told her that I should be fine in a couple of days. Turning to me, he said, "This won't taste very good, but trust me… if you do everything that I say, you'll get well." Before he left, he leaned over the bed and gave me a little hug. For a doctor, he was actually pretty nice, and he didn't even give me a shot! The medicine tasted awful, and I hated swallowing those aspirin, but Dr. Coker knew what he was talking about. By obeying his instructions, it wasn't long before I was back to my healthy, happy self!

Thinking back on that day and what Dr. Coker told me, I'm reminded of one of my favorite hymns. It goes like this: "Trust and obey, for there's no other way, to be happy in Jesus, but to trust and obey."

25

Captured by the Cattle Guard

When I was in third or fourth grade, one of the fun things to do in the summer was ride my bicycle up to the elementary school playground and play on all the equipment. No waiting in line. You could run from one thing to the other and have a blast. We had see-saws, a merry-go-round, a tall slide, a jungle gym, monkey bars, and the always exciting "johnny strikes." Most of you probably don't know what johnny strikes are because they began removing them from playgrounds a long time ago because everyone said they were dangerous. Us kids didn't think so. We just thought they were fun. Johnny strikes consisted of a tall metal pole with about ten or twelve chains hanging from a swivel at the top. At the end of each chain was a handhold that had two, short horizontal bars (one for each hand), and you could run fast in a circle, pull your feet up off the ground, and swing around in the air. The faster you ran, the higher you'd fly! One day, I got on my bike and rode up to the playground. There was a fence around the school, but there weren't any gates, just cattle guards. As I approached the cattle guard, I slowed down too much and over I went, falling right in the middle of it. As it happened, my skinny little leg and foot fell between the bars. When I bent my leg to pull it out, my foot came free, but my knee was stuck. I tugged and pulled, but it wouldn't budge. The harder I tried, the more stuck it became.

After a few minutes, I decided I needed help and began yelling, but no one was around. I began to get scared, thinking about how a car might come around the corner, turn into the playground and run right over me. I yelled louder and even began to cry. My knee was getting sore from all the pulling and yanking, and I was becoming very tired. Finally, I gave up, lay flat on the cattle guard, and cried, asking God to help me. Then a miraculous thing happened. As I lay there, weary and completely relaxed, my leg slid free from between the bars. While I had strained, pulled, and tugged, my leg had been flexed, making my knee bigger; but when I finally relaxed, and my leg was straightened out, my knee was smaller, and I was able to lift it free.

Reflecting on that childhood incident, I thought of something else. So many times, when something goes wrong in my life, or there is a crisis of some kind, I try to "fix" things on my own, usually resulting in something even worse. Why don't I ask God to help me in the first place? When will I ever learn?

Psalm 118:5 – "In my distress I prayed to the Lord, and the Lord answered me and set me free."

26

Frankie Dean's Geese

When I was growing up in Magnolia in the early 1950s, there was no stock law. That meant that cows, horses, pigs, chickens, and other animals roamed freely about the town. It was pure heaven for a kid who loved animals, except for one exception: Mr. Frank Dean's geese.

When I was as young as seven or eight years old, I was allowed to walk to T.H. Yon's Grocery Store all by myself. It helped that Papaw's house was right on the way and close to the store. Yon's Grocery was located where Chicken Express is today, and Mr. Frank Dean (Henry's grandfather) owned a grocery store right across the street, where Magnolia Foods is located now. He had a flock of geese that wandered all over town, but they usually hung around pretty close to home.

One day, as I walked to the store, I saw the geese between me and Mr. Yon's store. I picked up a rock and chunked it at them to make them go away, but if any of you know geese very well, you can imagine what happened next. Here they came, heads lowered, wings spread, bills wide open, hissing like the gates of hell had been opened. To a little girl of only a little over 3' in height, they looked like dinosaur geese! I turned around and ran as fast as I could toward Papaw's house, but one of them managed to grab the calf of my leg with its beak. OW! I never had anything hurt so bad!

From that day on, I planned my route around wherever those geese were. I carefully strategized each time I went to the store. First, I would carry a long stick for self-defense if they launched an attack. Then, I'd scout out their location from a safe distance and plan my route. My approach would be from a shed behind Papaw's house, then to an oak tree between his house and the store, and finally, a quick sprint to the back door of Yon's store. I had to be equally careful when I left, because I swear, if those geese saw me run in that back door, they'd be waiting for me when I left. Geese are smart like that. They also have very long memories.

Those geese and I had a long-running feud until one day I finally had enough. I stood and faced them squarely and told them I wasn't running any more. Bring it on, but bring it to my face because I wasn't running from them anymore. I had found a pretty good-sized stick on the way to the store, and I stood there and tried to look tall as they came at me with lowered beaks. When they got close, I raised my stick high and tried to look as mean and tough as I could, while inside I felt like jello. Swinging that stick in their direction, I began to feel pretty confident. Sure enough, they stopped just short of me and after an angry face-off, they turned and waddled away.

That was a proud moment for a little-bitty country girl. I had looked fear in the face, and I had won! Oh, we still had our moments, and we still didn't like each other, but I never ran from those geese again… and I always had my stick with me!

Nothing looks so bad when you face it as it does when you're running from it, and we who are God's very own children can face the scariest of situations with full confidence!

Deuteronomy 31:6 – "Be strong and of good courage, do not fear nor be afraid of them; for the Lord your God, He is the One who goes with you. He will not leave you nor forsake you."

Yep! I showed those geese who was boss!

27
Safe from the Storm

It was a very stormy night, and I was a scared six-year-old girl huddling under the covers. You should know that I prided myself in not being scared of much of anything—not snakes, bugs, spiders, horses, dogs, or even the bullies at school. If I couldn't make friends with them, I'd just stay away from them. The worst thing in the world to me at that age was if Jimmy called me a sissy. No way would I ever be a sissy!

This particular day had started out like most other days, with me riding my bike and playing with my friends. After supper, the family had gathered around the television to watch whatever great family shows were on that night. I enjoyed watching those shows, but when the news came on, I quickly got bored. I couldn't understand why my parents were always looking forward to the news and weather. *Boring!* Anyway, this particular night I did happen to hear that some thunderstorms were forecast for our area overnight. It didn't bother me; I just wanted it all to be finished by morning so it wouldn't interfere with my playing outside. Rainy days were the worst of times, and I was just glad this storm would be happening at night. Little did I know what was in store for me.

It had already begun to rain when I crawled into bed, and I fell asleep listening to the gentle raindrops landing on the roof. I felt so cozy and comfortable. Then… KABOOM! The loud clap of thunder sounded as though it was right at the foot of my bed. BOOM! BOOM! Again, and again, the thunder crashed, the wind raged, and the lightning lit up the room. I could actually see the shadows of tree limbs waving like monsters on my wall. Grabbing the covers, I pulled them over my head… although I couldn't see the monsters anymore, I could still hear the thunder. BOOM! POW! KABOOM! That last clap of thunder actually made my windows rattle.

That did it! Grabbing my pillow, I hit the floor running, and raced to my parents' bedroom. They were both awake, and must have been expecting me because as soon as I got to the side of their bed, my dad lifted the cover and said, "Crawl in!" I didn't just crawl in. I climbed over my dad and got between him and my mom. They both rolled over toward me and put their arms across me and hugged me tight. Nothing ever felt so good. "Everything's going to be fine, Tarvah. It's just a little storm and it will be over before too long, so don't worry," they assured me. The thunder still crashed, and the lightning still lit up the room, but I wasn't afraid anymore. Things were going to be okay, I was safe, and the trouble would soon be over. I knew it was true, because my parents said so. Snuggling down between them, wrapped safely in their arms, I soon fell fast asleep.

The next thing I knew, it was morning and the sun was shining. As I lay there between my parents, all fear was gone and all I could think about was what was for breakfast. (Some things never change!) I had also learned something very important. Any time I was afraid, all I had to do was find my parents, and everything would be okay!

Looking back, I can see that another lesson was learned without my even knowing it. My parents just modeled what God would do for me all my life. I can always go to Him, and I will always be safe in His arms.

Deuteronomy 33:27 – "The eternal God is your refuge, and underneath are the everlasting arms…"

Proverbs 18:10 – "The name of the Lord is a strong fortress; the godly run to him and are safe."

28

Corrected the Teacher

In 1951, during the Korean War, my dad was a radio man on the troop transport ship, the USS Magoffin. For a while it was in dry dock, so my mom, Jimmy, and I went to El Cajon, California for several weeks to be with him. When we got out there, Jimmy and I were quickly enrolled in school. Jimmy was in sixth grade, and I was in second grade.

After I had been there for a few weeks, our teacher, Mrs. Breeding, was printing an announcement on the blackboard. She was reminding us about an upcoming evening event at our school, and she quickly spelled "night" as "n i t e." Immediately, my hand shot up into the air. "What is it, Tarvah?" she asked. In my little Texas drawl, I innocently told her, "I don't know how y'all spell night in California, but in Texas we spell it 'n i g h t.'" I didn't stop to think about how it sounded… me correcting the teacher… and I really wasn't trying to be a smart aleck. I just wondered why she would teach the kids something wrong. Anyway, Mrs. Breeding patiently said, "You're right, Tarvah. That's the correct way to spell it and I shouldn't have been in such a hurry." She was very gracious, and even laughed when she later told my mom about it. It probably wasn't the right thing for me to do, but I guess I started out early in my life always wanting to know the truth. Come to think about it, that's exactly what God wants us to do. Seek the truth!

John 8:32 – "And you shall know the truth, and the truth shall make you free."

2 Peter 2:1-3 – "But there were also false prophets among the people, just as there will be false teachers among you. They will secretly introduce destructive heresies, even denying the sovereign Lord who bought them—bringing swift destruction on themselves. Many will follow their depraved conduct and will bring the way of truth into disrepute. In their greed these teachers will exploit you with fabricated stories. Their condemnation has long been hanging over them, and their destruction has not been sleeping."

Me, seated second row, first from left
My sweet teacher, Mrs. Breeding, standing back right

29
Rodeo on the Football Field

Back when I was in fourth or fifth grade, we had a rodeo on the football field at Magnolia High School. It was after football season, and they were going to disc up the field, so they must have decided that a rodeo would be a good way to get started. It was lots of fun to hang around and watch them build the chutes and pens and the fence that would go around the field. I planned on sitting on that fence so I could see the bull riders and the bronc riders up close and personal. I also had a little secret. One of my friends, Betty, lived on a ranch, and her family raised horses and cattle and all kinds of livestock. But there was one particular animal that I had in mind—a huge Brahma bull named Show Man. Show Man wasn't just any old ordinary bull. He was huge, and fat, and very mean-looking… but he was also gentle enough to ride. You could sit up there behind that big old hump and hang on and ride him all around the pen.

As most of you know, a rodeo gets started with a Grand Entry, which is a sort of parade that takes place inside the arena. Here was my secret—I wasn't planning on watching this parade—I was going to ride in it. I had talked to Betty, and she was going to ride Show Man in the Grand Entry, and she told me I could ride behind her. Wow! I couldn't wait to see the look on my parents' faces when I rode that big bull out into the arena. When the big night finally arrived, I could hardly contain my excitement. Show Man was put into the pen, and Betty and I climbed up on his back. One of her friends was on a horse in front of us, and he put a halter and rope on Show Man, and away we went, with him leading us in the Grand Entry parade! When we got out in the middle of the arena, I scanned the audience to see if I could find my mom. It wasn't that hard to spot her. She was the one standing up with her arms grasping her head and her mouth hanging open. I'll never forget the incredulous look on her face. It was priceless! However, there *was* a "price" to pay afterwards. Mom chewed me out pretty good after everything was over. She said that I should have told her ahead of time how gentle Show Man was and that I should have asked her for permission to ride him in the Grand Entry. She also told me that I could have been seriously hurt, no matter how tame Show Man was—that there were any number of things that could have spooked him or excited him enough to make him act up. I hadn't thought of that. He was so gentle and sweet, my mind couldn't comprehend the idea of him being dangerous at all.

Looking back, I can see that my little escapade could easily have turned into a tragedy. I'm so thankful that God sends His angels to watch over those of us who just blunder along doing things our own way.

Psalm 91:11 – "God will put his angels in charge of you to protect you wherever you go."

30

Frozen Grasshoppers

I started first grade in California while my dad was at the naval base in San Diego, so I'm going to blame a young California boy for an experience I had when my family attended a backyard picnic there. All of the kids were running around playing in one area of the yard, while the grown-ups were doing their thing in another area. The cold drinks were iced down in a huge washtub, and it was there that something interesting was taking place. A young boy a little older than me was catching grasshoppers and taking them over to the washtub. Curious, I went running over to ask him what he was doing. He told me to watch closely as he took out a huge chunk of ice. Holding the live grasshopper firmly between his thumb and forefinger, he placed it on the ground and put the ice on top of it. After a minute or so, he removed the ice and the grasshopper just lay there, stiff as a board. He then picked it up and showed me that it was dead and said that he had frozen it. Taking it over to one of the backyard lights, he held the grasshopper over the light bulb, and before long it began to squirm in his fingers. He then placed it in his open palm, and soon it jumped away. He told me he had killed it and brought it back to life. I was in awe. Then he told me that I could do the same thing, and if I tried it, I would find out for myself.

Even at this young age, I had a tender heart for animals, birds, and even insects, and I was very sensitive to their feelings. But this looked like so much fun! For the next half hour or so, I spent my time catching grasshoppers, freezing them, and "bringing them back to life" so they could jump out of my hand. I felt so important! Then I made the mistake of keeping a grasshopper under the ice too long, and no matter what I did, it remained limp in my hand. I had certainly killed it, and there was nothing I could do to revive it. That kid had lied to me! We weren't bringing anything back to life because the grasshoppers had never died in the first place. While I stood there looking down at the poor thing, I was overcome with remorse. I had played with the life of a living thing like it was nothing at all. For the first time in my life, I realized that something could live or die solely at my whim… even if it was only a lowly grasshopper. Needless to say, I didn't enjoy the rest of the picnic very much, but I had learned another lesson. Everything has a right to its life, no matter how large or small it is, and it isn't up to me to decide whether anything lives or dies. And, once something is dead, that is final. It can't be undone.

A few short years later, I learned that death wasn't final after all. Jesus made sure of that, by rising from the dead and promising eternal life to all who would believe in Him. At the tender age of nine, I went down the church aisle and asked Jesus into my heart. Death will never be final for me; it will be the beginning of an eternity with Him.

Isaiah 26:19 – "But those who die in the LORD will live; their bodies will rise again! Those who sleep in the earth will rise up and sing for joy! For your life-giving light will fall like dew on your people in the place of the dead!"

31

The Baby Goats

I enjoyed visiting Aunt Joyce and Uncle Ruel when I was a little girl. They weren't really my aunt and uncle. Uncle Ruel was my mom's cousin, but I called them "aunt" and "uncle." It was great fun going to their house because they had cows, and horses, and chickens and stuff. And they also had goats.

Those goats caused me to get in some big trouble when I was about six years old. I loved to watch the little goats play. Nothing seemed to enjoy life like a little goat. They'd be walking along and then suddenly start running and jumping for no reason at all. Sometimes they even jumped over each other!

One afternoon we had gone to visit Aunt Joyce, and as usual, I stayed outside wandering around and checking out all the animals. As I walked out toward the barn, I noticed something really strange. All the little goats were in a huge pen and their mothers were on the outside of the pen. The little kids were bleating and running around, and their mothers were making noises too. I stood there for a while trying to figure it all out, and then it hit me. The poor little goats had been separated from their mothers and that's why they were so upset! Those little goats were very lucky, because I knew just what to do. I made my way through the mother goats and unlocked the gate. As I swung it open the little goats ran out, the mother goats ran in, and I hid behind the gate trying not to get trampled. It was total chaos! There were big goats and little goats bleating and running and jumping everywhere. Oh, how wonderful it all was. There was great joy and happiness all around as mothers and little kids reunited. Pretty soon I heard a voice calling out my name, and it wasn't a happy voice. "Tarvah!" Aunt Joyce yelled. "What have you done?" I went running over to my mom and told her I had just let the little goats out to be with their mothers. Then I heard Aunt Joyce shout, "It took us two days to get all those goats separated and now we have to do it all over again!"

Needless to say, I was just a little anxious about everything as we got in the car to go home. My mom told me that she knew I was just trying to help the little goats, but that I needed to always ask an adult before making a big decision like that. She said that the baby goats needed to be weaned from being dependent on their mothers so they could learn to live like big goats. She then told me that I could have been badly injured, and that sometimes there are reasons for things happening that I wouldn't always understand, that things aren't always as they seem. I later learned that several of the little goats had escaped through the barbed wire fence and had gotten on the railroad tracks where they were hit by a train. My "act of kindness" turned out not to be so kind after all.

That's a big reality in my spiritual life today. Sometimes there are reasons for things that happen that I don't understand. When I feel a need to act, I need to go to the Lord for direction and wisdom. I could probably save myself and others a lot of grief.

Proverbs 12:15 – "The way of a fool is right in his own eyes, but a wise man listens to advice."

Proverbs 3:5-6 – "Trust in the Lord with all your heart and lean not on your own understanding; In all your ways acknowledge Him, and He shall direct your paths."

32

California Road Trip

Road trips were always a highlight of my childhood. No matter whether they were just day trips to Waco to visit my grandparents and cousins, or two-week vacations. There's one trip that stands out in my mind when I was about seven years old, and Jimmy was about twelve. We were going to travel a long distance to see some very good friends of my parents. Jack and Molly Smith lived way out in California, and in the early 1950s there was no interstate highway!

Jack and Daddy had served in the U.S. Navy together during WWII and the Korean War, and Molly and my mom had bonded to become almost like sisters. They also had a daughter, Gerri, who was Jimmy's age and a son, Mike, who was my age, so our families fit together pretty well. We only got to see them once every few years, but every Christmas we talked with them on the telephone for almost an hour. Anyway, this trip was a great undertaking, and we began planning for it weeks in advance. Oh, the things we would see and do! It was the topic of conversation at the supper table every night. My mom told us that during our visit we would be going up into the mountains where Molly's uncle had a cabin, and there would be lots of snow. I was so excited that I could hardly go to sleep at night, not only because of the snow and the mountains, but because Jack was my childhood hero, and I couldn't wait to see him again. We packed our car so full that the back floorboard was filled up even with the back seat, so there was no space left. That would work out just fine, because when my parents drove straight through the night, Jimmy and I could just spread out our blanket and pillow and sleep like we were in a real bed!

The day finally came when we were ready to go, and I remember when we pulled out of Magnolia and headed west, Daddy began singing, "California, here I come. Right back where I started from... Open up that Golden Gate, California, here I come." Well, I joined right in, singing at the top of my lungs, because I was born in California, and this was a very appropriate song for me to sing. When we finally got to Jack and Molly's, we all piled out of the car and everyone started hugging, kissing, laughing, and jumping around... everyone talking at the same time! Oh, it was grand! After a couple of days, we headed up to the cabin to spend a night or two, and just like Mom had said, there was lots of snow! The four of us kids had a blast with snowball fights and sledding down the mountainside. Once, we got to going so fast that we had to turn the sled over to keep from going right into the creek! It was one of the happiest times in my life, and the visit was over far too soon.

Now, I live in anticipation of another trip. A trip where the end will actually be the beginning and will last forever. A trip where I'll get to meet Jesus, a *real* Hero, face to face! A trip that will take me to a place I'll never have to leave. A trip that will culminate in a reunion that will produce hugging, kissing, and joyous laughter. Oh, the people I will see and the things I will do! "Open up that Golden Gate, Heaven, here I come!"

1 Corinthians 13:12 – "For now we see through a glass, darkly; but then face to face: now I know in part; but then shall I know even as also I am known."

1 Corinthians 2:9 – "But as it is written, Eye hath not seen, nor ear heard, neither have entered into the heart of man, the things which God hath prepared for them that love him."

Me, Gerri, Mike, and Jimmy… at the mountain cabin

33

Learned How to Shoot

I first learned how to shoot when I was about eight years old. At that time, my family owned the land that is now Dogwood Patches, a little over 300 acres. Papaw, my mom's father, had a .22 rifle that he let me use as he taught me how to shoot. He'd take Jimmy and me out to 'the tank', which is what we called the pond that's across the street from where I live now; the one by Hubbard and Vickey Williams' house. Seems like it was much bigger back then. It had a lot of mayhaw trees all around the back of the pond, and those mayhaw berries made delicious jelly!

Anyway, there were always plenty of targets to shoot at, but the ones he had me aim for most were the turtles. He said if we didn't keep them thinned out, they would eat all the fish. Actually, I think it was because he knew I'd have a really hard time ever hitting one. I'd patiently sit on the bank with the .22, waiting for a turtle to pop its head out of the water, and then, taking careful aim… "kapow!" Another near miss. Seems like I could never hit one. If you've ever shot at turtle noses when they poked up out of the water, you know what I mean. Immediately after the shot, they'd disappear, and the waiting would begin all over again. Jimmy, being thirteen years old, had a lot more success than I did at the time, but I finally got to where I could hit a turtle about as often as he did.

Papaw used the waiting periods to instruct me on how to hold the rifle steady and look down the barrel using the sight to line up my target. He'd tell me to squeeze the trigger gently and not to jerk it. He'd also tell us many stories while we sat on the bank waiting for a shot, and he kept Jimmy and I entertained with lots of tales of early Magnolia. I had a lot of fun on the bank of that pond with Papaw and Jimmy, and I treasure those memories.

Reflecting on those times, I realize that it wasn't all about the shooting practice; it was about the quality time spent with those I loved. Even better is quality time spent with Jesus, and time spent in His Presence is treasured indeed.

Psalm 16:11 — "You make known to me the path of life; in your presence there is fullness of joy; at your right hand are pleasures forevermore."

34

Playing Pigtail

"Hey, Tarvah... do you want to play baseball with us?" my brother asked. I was about eight years old, and it was my thirteen-year-old brother asking the question. He and his friends never wanted me to tag along with them, usually telling me to go away and leave them alone. So when he asked me if I wanted to play, I should have been a little suspicious. Despite that, I excitedly grabbed my glove, said yes, and followed him out the door. This was going to be fun!

I should have known better. Down to the school playground we went... me, Jimmy, and five or six of his friends. When we got there, I asked Jimmy what position I was going to play. "Well," he said, "We're going to play flies and skinners, and you're going to be the pigtail." I had never heard of that position before and thought he made it up just for me. Proudly, I asked where to go and he pointed to a spot out behind where second base and told me to go stand out there. My job was to retrieve the balls that were fouled off or hit past the other kids.

In the game of flies and skinners, there is a hitter and three or more fielders. The objective of the game is to become the hitter by catching flies (fly balls), and skinners (ground balls). Usually, you had to catch three flies and six skinners to become the hitter. Jimmy grabbed a bat, tossed the ball up in the air, and hit a hot ground ball toward one of his friends. The boy missed the ball and it went way out past him into the field. "That's your ball, Tarvah. Go get it!" Jimmy yelled. Off I ran to retrieve it. Wow, this was fun!

The next ball he hit was a foul ball and it went off in the other direction. Again, Jimmy shouted, "That's your ball too, Tarvah!" Once more, I chased it down and threw it back to him. Another boy then took Jimmy's place, and I continued my job as "pigtail".

After about thirty minutes of chasing baseballs all around the playground, I asked Jimmy when it would be my turn to bat. "Pigtails never get to bat, Tarvah. They just get the baseballs everyone misses and throw them back in to the batter." I finally began to realize why Jimmy and his friends wanted me to play with them. I was doing all the dirty work! But you know what? I really didn't mind that much because at least I was included in the group, and occasionally I even caught a fly ball or a grounder headed my way. Sometimes they would even brag on me and tell me what a good job I was doing, and that just made me work harder.

Then came my reward. Jimmy told me that since I had worked so hard, I could take a turn at bat. Oh, joy! Confidently, I picked up the bat, tossed the ball up in the air, swung… and missed! Quickly reaching down, I picked up the ball for another try. This time I hit a pretty good fly ball. Success! I had been practicing hard all by myself, just in case I got a chance to play and could show them what I could do. Practice paid off!!

Looking back on those times, I realize that all that running and throwing made me a better ball player. At that time, having my big brother and his friends smile at me and even brag on me a little was its own reward. That's what I need to do with my life here on earth… work at everything I do as if it's for the Lord and win his smile!

"…Winning the smile of God, brings it's delight!"

Colossians 3:23 – "Whatever you do, work heartily, as for the Lord and not for men."

I didn't mind playing pigtail!

35

Lesson of the Dart

There have been countless times throughout the years that I've brought about my own misery by rushing in "where angels fear to tread". This behavior has been an apt description of my actions for much of my life, creating many "life lessons." I was reminded of this in church one morning when the pastor asked a question: "Are you willing to start asking God before every decision, 'What is the right thing to do?'"

When I was about eight years old, we lived in a small rental house in town. Our home had burned down, and we rented this house until our new one could be built. My brother, Jimmy, was about thirteen years old, and he and Johnny Purvis had a clubhouse across the alley behind our house with a dart board. One day, they got bored with throwing the darts at a target and decided it would be more fun to go out in the alley and see how high they could throw the darts into the air. When I saw what they were doing, I went running down there to get in on the excitement. Despite many heated warnings from Jimmy to "get out of the way" and "go home," I just *had* to be in the middle of it all, running around in circles while the darts were in the air.

Then, lo and behold, a dart came hurtling down from the sky and stuck straight up in the middle of my head. Blood began to spurt, I screamed bloody murder, and Jimmy ran over and pulled it out. That only made it bleed more and made me holler louder. Jimmy said, "Don't tell mom. I'll fix it."

Don't tell mom? Was he kidding me? I headed up to the back door as fast as my little legs could carry me. I was sure that I was going to die, and Jimmy was going to be in big trouble! I was so surprised when I found out that he didn't get into trouble at all. After cleaning me up and disinfecting my head, Mom told me I shouldn't have been there in the first place. If I had asked her first, she would have warned me of the danger and told me not to go. But it looked like such fun, and I wanted to be in the middle of it. Therein lies my problem!

So many times in the past, I have impulsively rushed headlong into things without first seeking God's direction… most of the time, with disastrous results.

Isaiah 30:21 – "Whether you turn to the right or to the left, your ears will hear a voice behind you, saying, "This is the way; walk in it.""

36

Cloah Brown

During my school years, we went on many field trips, but there is one that stands out in my mind. In second or third grade, our teacher announced that we were going on a special field trip. The school bus would take us down to the Magnolia depot, where we would board the train and ride it all the way to Navasota. We were even going to the dime store to purchase a souvenir to remind us of our great adventure! I couldn't wait for the day to come! My best friend at that time was Joyce Post, and we spent the whole week talking about how fun the train ride would be.

The day finally arrived, and we marched in line to the school bus. Joyce and I were talking and giggling, making plans for the day. When we got to the depot, the day took a turn for the worse. Our teacher said we would be sitting in assigned seats, and she put me in a seat with Cloah Brown. Cloah was a new student in our class, and she was very quiet and shy. I hadn't gotten to know her very well yet. I don't think anyone had. With a frown, I plopped down next to Cloah, looking straight ahead. At least Joyce had been assigned a seat with someone she knew, but I was stuck with Cloah. I planned to hook up with Joyce again as soon as we got off the train.

My little pouty self just sat there for a while, and then I heard Cloah say, "This is going to be fun, isn't it?" She smiled her sweet little smile, and I mumbled, "I guess so." Then she asked if I'd ever ridden on a train before, so I told her about my grandfather being the depot agent and about hanging around the depot watching the trains come and go, but I had never ridden on one. I found out that she loved horses, and we started talking nonstop. By the time we got to Navasota, a new friendship was beginning. When we got off the train and began our walk to the dime store, I asked her if she wanted to pal around with Joyce and me. We had a great time looking at all the toys in the store, trying to find toys we wanted that didn't cost more than 25 cents. I occasionally caught a glimpse of our teacher, and each time I saw a little smile on her face as she watched us. I had sure been mad at her when we started this trip, but now I just gave her a smile right back. Cloah didn't stay at our school very long, and I don't remember if she finished out the year. But I do remember that I liked her a lot, and she was always sweet and kind. She reached out to a sulky, grumpy little brat who was treating her rudely, and as a result, I gained a new and special friend. Cloah may not know it, but she taught me a very valuable lesson about kindness that day that I will never forget.

Luke 6:31 – "And as ye would that men should do to you, do ye also to them likewise."

Cloah

37

A Special Place to Go

When I was a kid, I had a special, private place where I would go if I needed some time alone. There was this big oak tree in our yard with a curve in the trunk, and close by were several limbs that formed a small alcove. It was perfect. Sometimes, if I was sad or felt bad about something I'd done, I'd go there and cry until I felt better. If I just wanted to be by myself, I'd climb up and hide, with those branches and leaves shielding me from the outside world. It was my fortress and my refuge, where nothing could hurt me.

But then came the time when I was about six or seven years old, and my special place failed me. Brother Danny Jones was the preacher at the Methodist Church, and he had a nephew named Scooter. Since the church and the parsonage, where Brother Danny lived, were just up the road and across the street from my house, I always knew when Scooter was there. One day, when Scooter came to visit, we got together as usual to play. I don't completely recall what started it, but we began to argue, and Scooter pushed me. My right arm just took off, and my balled-up fist hit him right in the nose. Blood began to flow, Scooter began to cry, and I began to run.

Good grief! I had punched out the preacher's nephew! I ran all the way home and climbed up to my special place, shedding a few tears of my own. I just knew Brother Danny was going to tell my mom, I would be in *big* trouble, and Scooter would never be my friend again. I sat there for a long time, scared and crying, but it didn't help me feel any better. Climbing down from my refuge, I headed inside to do the only thing that would help—tell my mom everything. Still crying, I blurted out what I had done and told her that I hadn't meant to hurt Scooter, that I just hit him after he pushed me. She gave me a hug and told me everything would be fine, but I had to apologize to Scooter. We went back to the parsonage, and I made my apology. It was hard to do, but it was a little easier because Scooter had to apologize to me too. And guess what... we stayed friends!

Now I have a place to go that will never fail me: the everlasting arms of God.

Psalm 18:2 – "The Lord is my rock, my fortress and my deliverer; my God is my rock, in whom I take refuge, my shield and the horn of my salvation, my stronghold."

Proverbs 18:10 – "The name of the Lord is a strong tower: the righteous runs into it and is safe."

Scooter and me, a few years earlier

38

Shot Day

"Oh, no… Shot Day!" My mind shouted the words and my stomach felt like I had just swallowed a lead weight. I knew it the minute I opened the doors to the school, because the smell of alcohol filled the air. Oh, how I hated shot days. They were the worst.

Back when I was in elementary school here in Magnolia, the school nurse would give shots to all the kids two or three times during each school year. You could get out of taking them if your parents wrote a note, but mine never did, so I got my shots at school like most of the other kids. They took us by grade level, and the principal would announce over the intercom when it was each class's turn to go. "Ready for third grade," he'd say, and we'd all go out in the hall and line up outside the nurse's office, shifting from one foot to the other trying to hide our nervousness. It wasn't too bad when I was in first grade because we were the first class to go and we got it over with quickly. But, by the time I got to fifth or sixth grade we had to wait all day until just before school was out. It didn't help things at all that you could hear the little kids crying as they came out of the nurse's office. Let me tell you…there was *nothing* else on my mind all day but getting that shot. How in the world did the teacher expect us to concentrate on anything in class, when the "dreaded shot" was waiting? I couldn't even enjoy lunch (which was my favorite time of day) because my stomach was in knots from worrying.

At recess, instead of playing we'd just sit around and talk about it, wondering if it was going to hurt. But then when it was finally my turn, it wasn't nearly as bad as I'd hyped it up to be, and it was over with pretty quick. And sometimes, just before we lined up, my name was called among the ones who didn't need to take it because it happened to be one that was only needed every other year. I'd worried all day about something that didn't even take place. Isn't that the way with most things we worry about? Many times, the dreaded event doesn't happen and even when it does it's not as bad as we thought it would be. Corrie ten Boom once wrote, "Worry does not empty tomorrow of its sorrow, it empties today of its strength." And, I might add, it's joy. I'm finally learning to trust God's word that no matter what will come in my future, He'll take care of it and He'll take care of me too. So… why worry?

Matthew 6:27 (NLT) – "Can all your worries add a single moment to your life?"

Phil. 4:6-7 (NIV) – "Do not be anxious about anything, but in every situation, by prayer and petition, with thanksgiving, present your requests to God. And the peace of God, which transcends all understanding, will guard your hearts and your minds in Christ Jesus."

39

Helen Hunt Falls

There's a neat place near Colorado Springs where you can have a picnic and do a little hiking. It's called *Helen Hunt Falls*, and I visit it often in my mind. Here, an incident took place that is forever etched in the minds of my mom, my brother, and me. Our family was visiting the falls one summer when I was about eight years old, and Jimmy was about 13. Mom and Dad were packing up the remains of our picnic, so Jimmy and I decided to do a little looking around. Then, Jimmy had this neat idea. We would take a little hike and hide from our parents. What was I to do? He was my big brother, and I wasn't about to go against him (grin). Besides, it sounded like great fun. Sure enough, before too long we heard Mom calling, "Jimmeeeeee." "Tarvaaaah!" Snickering, we crouched down behind a big boulder. Soon, we saw her stepping over the rocks, headed down toward the stream, and of course looking for us instead of watching where she was going. First thing we knew, she slipped and landed on her rear. Oh, the joy of it all. This was much better than we expected! Bump, bumpitty, bump, down the rocks she went, bouncing along down toward the stream. Every time her bottom hit a boulder, her hair would fly up into the air. Our laughter could be heard all the way to Denver! Finally, she stopped her downward momentum, and we ran out from behind the rock to go help her up. She just sat there and glared at us. We couldn't help it, was just too funny and we couldn't hold it in. As we doubled over in laughter, she joined in, and a wonderful memory was created. We decided to give the place a new name, and thereby christened it "Celeste Graves Falls. Still brings a huge smile to my face.

But there's "Someone" you can never, ever hide from. The bad news is that we cannot hide our sins from God; but the good news is that He knew we would sin, so he sent Jesus into the world to pay for them in full. We're forgiven and we're loved, and no matter where we go, He will be with us always. Thank you, Father, that I am secure in your arms. Thank you, that you always know where I am.

Jeremiah 23:23-24 – "'Am I only a God nearby,' declares the Lord, 'and not a God far away? Can anyone hide in secret places so that I cannot see him?' declares the Lord."

Me, Mom, and Jimmy, near Helen Hunt Falls

40

The Donkey Bite

If you love animals like I do, you would have really enjoyed growing up in Magnolia in the early '50s. There was no stock law here then, so cattle, horses, donkeys, pigs, and chickens roamed freely throughout the town. My mom had warned me to be careful around the livestock, and not to take them for granted, but I assured her that they were my friends and they all loved me. However, there was this one experience that wasn't exactly enjoyable for me.

One morning, when I was about seven or eight years old, my mom sent me to the store. As I began walking up the road, I spotted one of my "friends" grazing in the vacant lot across from the Methodist Church. She was a sweet little donkey that I had petted often, and she would even let me hug her neck. Quickly, I went over to her and began petting her and scratching her between her ears. She loved when I did that and would hang her head low and close her eyes while I scratched away. As I stood there petting her, a neat idea popped into my head. I could just get on her back and ride her to the store! I had read where cowboys could guide their horses with their knees, so that's just what I would do. I grabbed her mane, stuck my toes (I was always barefooted in the summer) into that little hollow space behind her knee, and climbed aboard. When I was comfortably settled, I began kicking her in the ribs to make her go. She just stood there. I kicked harder and said, "Giddy up!" She just stood there. I jerked on her mane, kicked her even harder, slapped her on the neck and said, "Giddy up!" She looked around at me, shook her head, and stood there. By this time, I was getting a little upset because my plan wasn't working out too well. I decided to get off and get her started moving so that she would get the idea of what I wanted her to do. Walking up to her head, I put my hand beneath her jaw and started walking and trying to pull her forward. She just stood there. So, I jerked her a little harder. She didn't just stand there any more... she bit me. Turning her head toward me, she opened her mouth wide and clamped down on my forearm. As I stood there wailing, she shook her head again and began to graze as if nothing unusual had happened. I was crushed. My mom had warned me, but I wouldn't listen. I thought I knew the animals better than she did, but I could have sure saved myself some pain if I'd paid more attention to what she said. You can bet that I never tried to force my way on that little donkey again!

God Himself instructs us to listen and learn. We could save ourselves a lot of grief if we did just that!

Proverbs 4:1-2 – "Listen, my sons, to a father's instruction; pay attention and gain understanding. I give you sound learning, so do not forsake my teaching."

41

Jam Sessions

Some of the fondest memories of my early childhood involve music and singing. My dad loved to play the piano. He couldn't read a note of music, so he just played by ear, and he could play just about anything he set his mind to. One of my favorite stories about him was when his Aunt Maggie caught him playing "The Old Rugged Cross" boogie-woogie style on the piano when he was about 12 years old. I can just see him doing that. He said he got one of the worst whippings of his life! Daddy could also play the guitar and he had a real good voice. On many a Friday or Saturday night, Glynn and Johnny Taylor and Howard and Inez Davenport would come to our house for a "jam session." Oh, I so looked forward to those nights! Johnny played the accordion, Howard played the guitar, and Daddy would play the piano or the guitar while everyone joined in the singing. Most times when grownups came over, Jimmy and I were not allowed to hang around, but when the jam session was in progress, we were right in the middle of it. Many of the songs were the popular Hank Williams, Bob Wills, Woody Guthrie, Ernest Tubb, etc., tunes of the day, and at the ripe old age of eight I knew them all by heart. "Stay all night, stay a little longer. Dance all night, dance a little longer. Pull off your coat, throw it in the corner. Don't see why you can't stay a little longer." Everyone would gather around the piano, and we would all sing our hearts out. In between songs there was lots of laughter. One of Ernest Tubbs' songs always put a funny image in my head. "I'm walking the floor over you. I can't sleep a wink, that is true." In my childish mind I would picture a man walking back and forth on the floor over his wife who was lying under the house! What grand and happy times! Daddy even bought me a small accordion of my own and I actually learned to play along with a few songs. The only time I got a little uncomfortable was when they tried to get me to sing by myself. Nope! THAT wasn't happening! They would sometimes trick me by letting me join in and then they'd suddenly quit singing and I'd sing a few words by myself before I could stop. They really got a kick out of that! Now these jam sessions weren't just short little episodes. They would last for hours, with an occasional break for snacks and cokes or coffee. That singing would go on late into the night, and Jimmy and I would head off to bed and listen from our bedrooms until we drifted off to sleep. Sometimes I could stay awake long enough to hear the Woody Guthrie song they always closed with: "So long, it's been good to know yuh; … and I got to be driftin' along."

They sang "The Old Rugged Cross" at Daddy's funeral, and I have to smile just a little, thinking about how he played it when he was a kid. I'm thinking the chorus of the Woody Guthrie tune wouldn't be so bad to sing at a funeral either; especially if Heaven is your next stop. "So long, it's been good to know yuh….and I got to be driftin' along."

Hebrews 13:14 – "For this world is not our permanent home; we are looking forward to a home yet to come."

42

The Shortest Psalm

"Tarvah, it's your turn to read tonight." These words came from my mom and, as an eight-year-old, I was prepared.

Every night in our home, my family read the Bible together before bedtime. I'll have to admit, I didn't really enjoy it and thought it was kinda boring. We read from the King James version, and sometimes it was hard for me to understand. We would gather around in my parents' bedroom, and someone would read a chapter aloud. At first it was usually my dad or my mom, but as Jimmy grew older, he began to take his turn. Now it was my turn. I knew it was coming, so, like I said, I was prepared. I had picked one of the shortest chapters that I could find. Psalm 100. I had it marked, so it was easy and quick for me to find. Hesitantly, I opened my Bible and began to read, gaining confidence as I neared the end. Everyone smiled at me when I had finished. Well…. Mom and Dad smiled… Jimmy just kinda looked at me with that look that only he could give. After all, he was 13 and a very accomplished oral reader, so his look was just a little smug. Anyway, now I had taken my place in the rotation, and felt like I was an important part of the family devotional time! From that time on, whenever it was my turn, I would look ahead and pick one of the shortest Psalms. Psalm 100 quickly becoming my "go to" chapter, but Psalm 23 was a very close second!

I treasure those memories and have learned to appreciate the fact that my parents made a daily devotional an important part of our lives. My mom told me that she and her parents had a period of Bible reading together when she was growing up, and she incorporated it into our lives. That practice became ingrained in me, and as a result it later became a regular routine for my own family with my own children. We read our Bible together every night. Even if sometimes it was only the very shortest Psalm!

Psalm 100:5 – "For the Lord is good. His unfailing love continues forever, and his faithfulness continues to each generation."

43

Dubie Mixon

When I was in third grade, Mary Shannon started school in Magnolia and became my very best friend. We were both tomboys, so naturally we had a lot of things in common like playing football and baseball, climbing trees, riding horses, and yes, even wrestling. At recess, we were always in the middle of the boys' football games or baseball games (whatever the season), and I can honestly say we held our own against the guys! Back then all 12 grades were on the same campus, right on Main Street in Magnolia. The school cafeteria was a large, white, wood-framed building and it sat right behind the elementary classes, so the high school kids would walk past our playground to go eat lunch. There was this one high school boy, Dubie Mixon, who was a star player on the football team, and I thought he was really cute. It just so happened that our recess time was the same time he went to lunch, so every day I would manage to be close to the cafeteria when he walked by. I began trying to think of some way to get him to notice me and came up with a great plan to show him how tough I was. It would depend on Mary's cooperation, but what were friends for if not to help a pal look good? The next day when we saw Dubie coming, we got in his line of sight and started wrestling. I pushed Mary to the ground, and we began rolling around in the dirt. We timed it just right, so that when he got really close, I had her pinned. Mary, being the really GOOD friend that she was, began hollering "calf rope" at the top of her lungs, and I gave her my fiercest look as I held her shoulders to the ground. This was really going well. Then, to my great humiliation I heard him say to his friends as they were walking by, "Did you see that mean little girl?" I was totally mortified. Things definitely did not go as planned, and I just wanted to crawl into a hole somewhere. Needless to say, from that time on I made it a point to be as far away from the cafeteria as possible when Dubie Mixon went to lunch.

Another hard lesson learned. Nothing good can come of trying to impress people in this world; especially if you have to do something out of character to do it. As I grew older, I began to understand that my main focus in this life should be to show God how much I love Him by the way I act. I fail many times…but it's still my goal. "Winning the smile of God, brings its delight!"

Colossians 3:23 – "And whatsoever ye do, do it heartily, as to the Lord, and not unto men…"

44

The Day Our House Burned

The first time I realized a grown-up would lie stands out very clearly in my mind. I was an eight-year-old third grader, and I was standing by the side of the road watching in horror as our home burned to the ground.

The day started out just like any other day. My dad was a traveling salesman for Strauss Bodenheimer, and he had just left to go on the road that morning as my mom, and Jimmy and I got dressed and went to school. About the middle of the morning, I was on the playground at recess, and someone said, "Look at all that smoke!" We lived just a couple of blocks from the school, and as I looked toward the smoke, I realized that it was our house burning. With my heart in my throat, I left the playground and raced down the street as fast as my legs would carry me. When I got there, I saw Auntie standing by the road with tears in her eyes, and then my mom and Jimmy arrived from school. My mom was friends with Pauline, the telephone operator who was stationed in Tomball, and Pauline knew that my dad sold leather goods. She also knew that one of his stops that morning would probably have been at Froelich's Feed Store, just west of Tomball. Sure enough, when she called the store, he was still there and that's how he got the news.

The next thing I remember is standing by my parents watching my mom cry, and then I began crying too. It was very frightening to see our house burning, but I was also upset because of my stuffed dog. He was about half the size I was, and I slept with him every night. We had a two-story home, and my bedroom was upstairs next to my parents' room. That's where the fire started, in the upstairs attic, and the flames were leaping high from the roof and upper floor when I got there. Soon, most of the high school kids arrived as well and were running in and out of the house trying to save anything they could. The closest fire station was in Tomball, and strangely enough, Magnolia's first fire engine arrived in town that very afternoon…. too late to do anything about our home.

Now, back to the reason for my story. As I stood there crying, a man I had never seen before heard me tell my parents that I hoped someone had saved my stuffed dog. He immediately bent down and said to me, "Don't cry. I saw someone throw your dog out of the upstairs window. You can probably find him after all the flames are out." Well, his words stopped my crying, but they also wound up causing me a lot more grief later. You see, I hunted all over for that dog after the fire was out. I even asked several people if they had picked him up or seen him anywhere. It took a few days before the reality sank in and I knew my little stuffed friend hadn't made it.

To this day, I can see that man bending over and telling me that lie. I know he meant well, but he had only given me false hope, and sadly I also remember him as "the man that lied." At a very young age, I discovered that people can't always be trusted. But there is One who never lies, and in Whom we can have complete assurance.

Psalm 91:2 – "I will say of the Lord, He is my refuge and my fortress: my God; in him will I trust."

Psalm 18:2 – "The Lord is my rock, and my fortress, and my deliverer; my God, my strength, in whom I will trust; my buckler, and the horn of my salvation, and my high tower."

My dad, with his hand over his eyes, holding the hose, watching our house burn

45

The Stringer that got Away

Papaw was serious about his fishing, and if you wanted to go with him, you'd better be serious about it too. He didn't put up with any shenanigans or foolishness, like chunking rocks at his cork, or slamming your fishing line overhanded out onto the water to make your cork land real hard on the water. Nope... fishing with Papaw was serious business.

One afternoon, when I was about six years old, he told me we were going out to Mr. Seyle's place to fish. Roscoe Seyle was a friend of his who owned some land with a small lake right by where Wistaria Farms is located now. Pap had always used a long cord with a metal shaft on the end as a stringer, but he proudly showed me a new one he had just bought, made of shiny metal with lots of individual clips attached. Off we went to Mr. Seyle's place to catch our supper. Papaw sure knew how to fry up fish, and I could hardly wait.

Of course, he began to catch fish right away, but I spent more time chasing grasshoppers for my bait than I did fishing. For some reason, my fingers just couldn't get those slippery worms on the hook, but I had no such problem with grasshoppers. Pretty soon Pap's stringer was almost full, and I had actually contributed a few perch myself. It had been a long time since I had caught anything, though, and I was beginning to get a little bored. Papaw was over on the other side of the lake, so I decided it would be a good time to take a look at how many fish we had caught. I slowly pulled the stringer out of the water and lifted the fish to count them. There were so many I could hardly lift them up. Carefully, I put them back in the water and stuck the metal tip in the ground to stake them out. To my horror the metal tip quickly began slipping out of the ground and the fish swam away. I had staked them in really soft mud, and they had easily pulled it out. Frantically, I grabbed at the stringer, but it was too late. There was nothing I could do but watch. I slowly walked back over to my pole and acted like I was fishing, but really, I was only thinking about what I was going to tell Papaw.

Soon Pap came back over to where I was and said we would have to leave if we were going to have time to clean the fish and cook them for supper. My stomach began to hurt. Going to where he had staked them out, he began looking all around. "Isn't this where I put the stringer?" he asked. Oh…. I so wanted him to think he was the one who had messed up, but I just couldn't do it. "It was my fault, Papaw," I blurted out. "I pulled them out to look at them and when I put them back in the water, I stuck the stake into the soft mud, and they all got away. I'm sorry!" At first, he got a real angry look on his face, and then he saw the tears begin to form in my eyes. Slowly, he put his arm around me and told me it was okay, that he knew I didn't mean to do it, but next time to be sure to stake them in hard, dry ground.

Well, we went home empty-handed, but I felt good knowing that Papaw loved me anyway. About a week later, Mr. Seyle called Papaw and told him he had his stringer. He had spotted it at the edge of the lake with a few fish heads and bones still attached. It seems the turtles had enjoyed their own fish supper.

I can still recall how good it felt to know that Papaw had forgiven me and that it didn't change his love for me one bit. That's just how I feel now, knowing that God does the same thing. How blessed I was as a child to have adults in my life who modeled God's love for me.

1 John 1:9 – "If we confess our sins, He is faithful and just to forgive our sins and cleanse us from all unrighteousness."

Papaw forgave me for the stringer

46

Pabst Blue Ribbon

Television can be both a blessing and a curse. I think in today's culture it's more of a curse, but that's another story.

My dad was a salesman for Motorola back when I was in second or third grade, so our family was fortunate enough to have one of the first televisions in town. As a result, a lot of my friends showed up at our house after school and on Saturdays. We enjoyed watching the shows but those commercials, even then, really captured our attention. Most of them involved a song, and we would find ourselves singing along with them. "Northern Tissue, Northern Tissue… two good reasons why. Northern Tissue, Northern Tissue… is your very best buy." "What'll you have? Pabst Blue Ribbon! What'll you have? Pabst Blue Ribbon! What'll you have? Pabst Blue Ribbon. Pabst Blue Ribbon beer!" That last one got me in a little bit of trouble.

Back when I was in third grade, Ma and Pa Williams had a café on the corner of Main Street catty cornered from the elementary school. At lunchtime, students were allowed to leave campus and walk across the parking lot to the cafe if we had our parents' permission. At this point, you need to know that my parents were staunch members of Magnolia Baptist Church, and they didn't drink. Well, one day I sauntered into the café and climbed up on one of the bar stools to order my hamburger. Ma came over to me and said, "Hi Tarvah. What'll you have?" What did she just say? Oh, boy…Ma was going to love this! Putting on my biggest grin, I slapped my hand down flat on the counter and the words tumbled out of my mouth. "Pabst Blue Ribbon!" I could just imagine how hard Ma would laugh, but to my chagrin, she didn't. Drawing her eyebrows together in a huge frown, Ma said, "Tarvah Graves. You should be ashamed of yourself. What will your parents think?" I noticed she didn't say what WOULD they think; she said what WILL they think, so I knew they were going to hear about this. Well, I went ahead and ordered my hamburger, but I didn't enjoy eating it very much.

After school, I told Mom what I had said because I knew she'd be hearing about it from Ma sooner or later. That's how it was in Magnolia back then. This "It takes a whole village to raise a child" saying didn't have anything on Magnolia! Anyway, Mom sat me down and explained to me that even though I had just been joking, the way I behaved in public was a reflection on my family and our family life. I hadn't thought about it that way, but this whole episode made me sit up and take notice. I was proud of my family, and I sure never wanted to do anything to embarrass them!

Now I belong to another Family, and I try hard to live in a way that won't bring shame to my Heavenly Father. "I'm so glad I'm a part of the Family of God, I've been washed in the fountain, cleansed by His blood! Joint heirs with Jesus as we travel this sod, For I'm part of the family, The Family of God."

1 John 3:10 – "By this it is evident who are the children of God, and who are the children of the devil: whoever does not practice righteousness is not of God, nor is the one who does not love his brother."

Russell Salmon, Ma and Pa Williams, and Aunt Cynthia (Ma's sister)
My place of shame was at the counter in the swivel chair on the far left.

47

Avey Mae Christmas

When I was in second grade, a new girl joined our class at Magnolia Elementary School. Her name was Avey Mae Christmas. She had long, dark, curly hair and she always wore long dresses. I thought she was very pretty, but it was her name that fascinated me the most. I thought it was beautiful, and I loved to say it. It just kind of rolled off your tongue. *Avey Mae Christmas.*

Avey Mae didn't make friends very quickly because she was so shy, and I think my boisterous group was a bit too much for her. On our playground back then, there were lots of things to play on. We had swings, johnny strikes, a huge slide, seesaws, a merry-go-round, and a jungle gym. The bunch I played with got pretty rowdy sometimes and would do some things that weren't very smart. We liked to run down the slide, and we would get the merry-go-round going really fast and jump off to see if we could hit the ground running and not fall down. We also liked to stand on one end of a seesaw and run up it until the other side would crash to the ground. And when we were seesawing with someone, it was great fun to have another kid jump on your end with you to make the person on the other end fly up into the air. Stupid stuff like that. Our teacher, Mrs. McPherson, would constantly warn us about the danger of getting hurt or hurting someone else, but it just made us mad that she didn't want us to have any fun.

Anyway, one day at recess I saw Avey Mae seesawing with one of my classmates. As they happily went up and down, one of my friends went running over and jumped on the opposite end of the seesaw from Avey Mae. It slammed to the ground, and we all began grinning as she went flying high into the air, the skirt of her long dress blowing in the wind. To my horror, she didn't land back on the board, but instead went crashing to the ground letting out a loud wail. Then she just kept on crying. We all ran over to see if she was okay, but she wasn't. She had broken her arm. Gosh, our teacher had warned us that something like this could happen. Mrs. McPherson quickly came over and carried Avey Mae into the nurse's office where they waited for her mom to come and take her to the doctor.

Back in the classroom Mrs. McPherson pointed out to us that sometimes it's the person who's completely innocent that pays for the misdeeds of others. There was Avey Mae, playing happily and safely like she was supposed to, and she was the one who got hurt as a result of someone else's rowdiness. The next day Avey Mae came to school with her arm in a cast and quickly became the center of attention. We fell all over ourselves doing things for her…sharpening her pencils, opening her paste jar, helping her with her lunch, and just about anything she asked us to do. Suddenly she was the most popular kid in our class and I think she really enjoyed the attention. I'll always remember Avey Mae Christmas. I wonder what she's doing today…

When we're young, we have so much to learn about life and its dangers. That's why we need to be taught, but teaching won't be fruitful unless we listen!

Proverbs 19:20 – "Listen to advice and accept discipline, and at the end you will be counted among the wise."

Proverbs 12:15 – "The way of a fool is right in his own eyes, but a wise man listens to advice."

48

Little Green Man

I came very close to being abducted by aliens when I was in third grade. Little did my mom know when she tucked me in bed that night, that it could have been the last time she would conduct that nightly ritual. It seems like my eyes had barely closed when I saw it. Drifting slowly down out of the night sky was a small, white parachute, and dangling just below it was a little green man. As I watched in awe, he gently dropped to the ground…. right in our front yard! Untangling himself from the parachute, he stood there looking all around, and then he folded the chute and began to wander around the yard. He wasn't your typical, scary-looking, slant-eyed alien that you see in the movies; he was just a normal-looking, little bitty man. The only thing weird about him was that he was green. He kept searching around the yard, and he looked like he was looking for something (or someone).

I don't remember getting out of bed, or going outside, but suddenly I was standing outside in the middle of the yard with my eyes wide open. I think it must have been the only time I walked in my sleep. I do remember looking all around, but there was no little green man to be seen anywhere, so I walked up on the porch to go back in the house. I tried to turn the knob, but the door had locked behind me, so I knocked loudly and called for someone to come let me in. You should have seen the look on my mom's face when she opened the door and saw me standing there, in the wee hours of the morning, barefooted and in my pajamas. With a frown on her face, she loudly asked, "Tarvah, what in the world are you doing out there?" I tried to tell her about the little green man, but she just rolled her eyes, caught me by the arm, and "gently" led me back to bed. As she tucked me in again, she cautioned me to never go outside at night without asking someone first. Before I went to sleep, I thought about that little green man and wondered who he was looking for. In my wild imagination, I began to think it might have been me he was coming after, and I pulled the covers up over my head and tightly squeezed my eyes shut. I didn't want to see him again, and I sure didn't want him taking me anywhere!

Thinking back on this experience, I'm reminded of the rapture. If I'm still alive when the Lord comes down from Heaven to claim His own, I won't be covering my head and closing my eyes, and I won't be afraid. I will be shouting with joy as He takes me up to meet Him in the air!

1 Thessalonians 4:17 – "Then we which are alive and remain shall be caught up together with them in the clouds, to meet the Lord in the air: and so shall we ever be with the Lord."

49

Memories of Mamaw

I don't remember a whole about my Mamaw since she went home to Heaven only eight days before my fourth birthday, but the memories I do have are very precious to me. I remember that she was quite buxom, and there was a time when I was crying, and she picked me up and sat in a rocking chair and gently rocked me as she held me close to her heart. I remember how comfortable it was, and how safe and secure I felt as she held me in her arms and my tears quickly dried. There was another time when I had been outside playing and I got really hot and thirsty. I went into the kitchen (because that's where she always seemed to be) and asked for a drink of water. Mamaw took down the aluminum dipper and filled it with fresh cool water that was pumped into their house from the well in their back yard. Nothing ever tasted so good. Then again, there was a time I was spending the night with my grandparents, and it was cold and raining. Mamaw took me into their bedroom and placed me in her big feather bed and covered me with a soft warm quilt. I really didn't need the quilt because I sank so far down in that soft feather mattress that it almost folded over my body. I was so warm and comfortable as I lay there listening to the rain tap, tap, tapping on the tin roof, and I quickly went to sleep. I rested, safe and secure. In my mind I can still see Mamaw standing at the wood stove in her kitchen as she fixed my breakfast. I was so hungry and could hardly wait for her to finish. She made the best biscuits that just melted in your mouth when you filled them with her homemade butter. My hunger was quickly satisfied. One of the best memories I have is of Mamaw sitting in her rocking chair with her glasses on, reading her Bible. That Bible is now one of my most precious possessions.

Thinking back, I can clearly see how Mamaw modeled her Lord as she met my every need, and I realize the impact she had on my life in just those four short years. I truly believe that those memories had a part in leading me to the same Jesus that she knew and loved. Now He holds me close and I feel safe in His arms. He comforts me and dries my tears. He quenches my thirst with

Living Water. He feeds me with His Holy Word. But most of all, He loves me unconditionally. I know Jesus gave Mamaw a huge hug when she went home to be with Him. Yes, I remember Mamaw, and I want to be just like her!

Proverbs 31:10; 31:26-28 – "Who can find a virtuous woman? for her price is far above rubies. She openeth her mouth with wisdom; and in her tongue is the law of kindness. She looketh well to the ways of her household, and eateth not the bread of idleness. Her children arise up, and call her blessed; her husband also, and he praiseth her."

Mamaw, Jimmy, and me

50

In the Stall with Sam

When I was growing up in Magnolia, Uncle Ruel and Aunt Joyce Sanders lived in town on some land where the new Tractor Supply now stands. Uncle Ruel was my mom's cousin and Aunt Joyce was her best friend, so we spent a lot of time over at their house. I really liked going over there because Uncle Ruel had cows and horses and chickens and goats and stuff. All the things a kid likes to be around. He had this one horse I really liked; a feisty, black stallion named Sam. Aunt Joyce had warned me repeatedly not to pet him because he was mean. Well...he WAS mean to Aunt Joyce. I think it was because she was a little afraid of him, so she didn't like him very much. Horses can tell about things like that, you know, so he didn't like her very much either. Whenever she was around him, he'd try to bite her, but he never tried to bite me when I'd sneak around and pet him through the fence. I loved Sam, and I think he loved me too. One day when I was about five or six years old, Aunt Joyce was babysitting me, and I was playing outside. I went out to the barn and discovered that Uncle Ruel had put Sam in a stall. Oh, this was wonderful! Now I could pet him and talk to him all I wanted, and no one would see me. I knew Sam enjoyed our visits, because he'd let me stroke him on his nose and he listened to everything I said. He'd look at me with those huge brown eyes and flick his ears when I talked. Well, Sam and I had been visiting for a while when I heard Aunt Joyce call me. Gosh, I couldn't let her see me come out of the barn because she'd know I'd been with Sam. I hoped she'd just go back in the house and wait for me to come in, but no, that wasn't to be. "Taaarvah," she called, as she began walking toward the barn. The only thing I could think of was hiding until she went back into the house, and the best place available was Sam's stall. I quickly opened the stall door and went inside with Sam, closing the half-door behind me. I went all the way to the back of the stall and crouched down on the floor. Sam just stood there craning his neck, looking back at me. Here came Aunt Joyce, right to Sam's stall. She seemed to know just where to look for me. "Tarvah," she cried, "You get out of there right now. Sam is going to stomp on you!" She had this scared look on her face. "Sam won't hurt me. He's my friend," I told her. She reached for the door latch and Sam stretched his neck out and snapped at her hand. I decided I'd better do what she said before something bad happened, so I got up, patted Sam on his side, and told him I had to leave. He just calmly watched me as I walked by and opened the stall door. Aunt Joyce didn't spank me, but she sure gave me a good talking to. She told me that grownups know more about danger than little kids, and that I needed to listen when I was warned about doing something that might get me hurt. My little escapade turned out fine that day but looking back now I can see that my disobedience could easily have ended in tragedy. How many times could we save ourselves pain and hurt by heeding God's warnings? God, Himself, asks us that question.

Luke 6:46 – "Why do you call me, 'Lord, Lord,' and do not do what I say?"

51
Selling Christmas Cards

When I was about eight or nine years old, I saw an ad in a magazine about how to make some extra money selling Christmas cards. Sounded like a great idea, so I talked to my mom about it, and she said it was fine with her, but I'd have to do the work myself. Hey, no problem! At a profit of 25 cents a box, I could get rich! I filled out the form and mailed it off as quickly as I could and began to watch the mail for my packet.

When it finally arrived, I saw that there was a little more to it than just selling a few boxes of cards. The packet consisted of a few sample boxes, some individual cards stuck to the pages of a huge album, some ledger sheets to place the orders on, a packet to put all the money in that I collected, and another envelope to put everything in to mail back. Gosh, there sure was a lot of stuff to keep up with, but I couldn't wait to get started. Of course, my mom got first pick of all the cards, and then I set off down the street pulling the album and all the other items behind me in my red wagon. I went all the way to the end of the street and knocked on Mrs. McTigrit's door. I had a great sales pitch, talking about how pretty the cards were, and saying that you couldn't find any like them in a store, etc. From there, I went across the street knocking on Papaw's door, then on to Mrs. Ware's and back across the lot by the church down to Auntie's house. My stop there lasted a little longer because she had teacakes and milk, and by that time I needed a little fortification. The wagon full of stuff was getting heavier by the minute. "Which cards have already been sold," Auntie asked me. "I don't want to get the same ones everyone else does." Well…I found out in the next few stops that this would become a regular question and the unique choices were getting fewer. I slowly trudged on down the road and knocked on Mrs. Yon's, door. My sales pitch was getting shorter. "Miss Hattie (that's what I always called her), you wanta buy some Christmas cards?" I quickly asked. After knocking on a few more doors, I finally headed back home. This door-to-door stuff was hard on the arms and legs!

Then Mom drove me around to some houses that were too far to walk to, and my knuckles began to get sore from so much knocking. I also began to hear a different phrase: "I wish you had started with me because someone has already ordered the best cards." This wasn't nearly as much fun as I had thought it would be. People sure were picky. What difference did it make if a few people got the same cards they sent out? Then came the paperwork. Each order had to be filled in, along with the number of boxes and the amount for each box, and then the total amount due from that person. When I finally finished doing that, I realized that I also had to figure the entire total of the order and make sure the money I had collected equaled the money that was owed. Good grief! By the time I had finished with all that I was pretty sick of cards of any kind. With a huge sigh of relief, I finally sent the order off in the mail, but I found out my work still wasn't done. Soon, a huge shipment arrived, and I had to sort out all the boxes, compare them with the orders, and get them delivered. Mom drove me to the far away houses, and then I set off out down the street again to make my deliveries, this time with boxes piled high in my red wagon. The end of that day didn't come soon enough for me. My profit of a little over $4.00 sure didn't seem to be worth all the hard work I had put in. This door-to-door selling just wasn't my cup of tea!

There's another One who knocks on doors, but He doesn't have anything to sell. What He offers is free and it isn't just for temporary pleasure; it's a life-changing experience and the reward goes on forever. I'm so glad I opened my door to Jesus and asked Him into my heart!

Revelation 3:20 – "Behold, I stand at the door and knock; if anyone hears My voice and opens the door, I will come in to him and will dine with him, and he with Me."

John 10:9 – "I am the door. If anyone enters by me, he will be saved …"

"Wanna buy some Christmas Cards?"

52

Barbecue and Beans

Ever since I can remember, barbecue and pinto beans have been some of my favorite foods, but there was one time in my life that I didn't enjoy them so much. Our school used to have a Halloween carnival on the football field every year and the entire town would turn out. There were all kinds of food booths, game booths, a cake walk, costume contests…and barbecue!

One year when I was about seven or eight years old, my friends and I had participated in just about everything at the carnival and had become rather bored. Kids get bored easily, you know. Anyway…one of the things we decided to do was to follow some of the older boys around and try to make their lives miserable. Actually, just by following them around we made them miserable but when we called them names or made fun of them with their girlfriends, they got sick of us pretty quick. We would make "cute" remarks and run away before they could reach out and grab us. It was great fun! There was one particular boy (I remember him well but won't mention his name) who got very aggravated at me. I had been taunting him for a long time, but finally decided to quit and go get something to eat. I got my plate of barbecue and beans and as I headed for a table to sit down with my friends, I just happened to pass him with his girlfriend. Unable to resist, I opened my mouth again with another smart remark…and paid the price. Before I knew what was happening, he reached out, grabbed my plate, and proceeded to smear the beans and barbecue (which was covered with sauce) all in my face. Horrified, I just stood there for a minute as he laughed, and then to my immense shame I began to cry. Only one thought popped into my mind: "Daddy!" Turning around, I ran as fast as I could, calling for Daddy as I wiped the gooey mess from my face. When I found him and told him what had happened, he immediately began to search for that unfortunate young man. Finding him quickly, Daddy chewed him out pretty good, but I was too far away to hear what he said. For some reason, I had lost interest in being anywhere around that boy. When it was all over and I was cleaned up, Daddy gave me a hug and said to me, "Tarvah, he told me what you and your friends have been doing, and you brought that on yourself. When you go looking for trouble, you're going to find it. I hope you've learned your lesson." Well, I wish I could say that I did learn my lesson but being the hard-headed person that I am the lessons have just kept coming. One thing I HAVE learned though… there is One I can always run to in times of trouble!

Psalm 18:2 – "The Lord is my rock, and my fortress, and my deliverer; my God, my strength, in whom I will trust; my buckler, and the horn of my salvation, and my high tower."

Psalm 59:16 – "But I will sing of your strength, in the morning I will sing of your love; for you are my fortress, my refuge in times of trouble."

53

This is my Story

"This is my story; this is my song." As we sang the chorus of "Blessed Assurance" in our church service one morning, I was reminded of a story-telling time of my own.

When I was growing up, some of the highlights of my life were when Auntie would read stories to me. When I was little, I would snuggle up in her lap, and then when I got too big for that, I would sit by her side on the couch or even lie on the floor at her feet. Many precious moments were spent on adventures with Uncle Wiggily or Billy Whiskers, and I loved the tales of Jimmy Skunk, Sammy Jay, Bobby Raccoon, and Reddy Fox in "Old Mother West Wind." I was held in suspense when young Balser had many frightening experiences with the bears in the forest where he lived, as Auntie would read from "The Bears of Blue River." But I had almost as much fun telling these stories to the little kids in my neighborhood as I enjoyed having them read to me. It was so neat watching their faces as I could make them laugh or feel scare, whatever the situation called for. However, I remember one time when telling a story didn't come so easily to me.

I was in third or fourth grade, and I decided I wanted to participate in the UIL "Story Telling" competition that was going to be held at our school. Since I really enjoyed telling stories, it seemed like this would be a slam-dunk for me to win first place. All the contestants gathered in one room while a teacher read a story to us. The idea was that each of us, one at a time, would then re-tell the story to an audience. As we spoke, we would be evaluated on how well we told the story, how completely we told it, and how interesting we made it to those who were listening. Hey, I had this! Hadn't I always been able to entertain my little friends with my stories? I could already picture the spot in my room where I'd hang that blue ribbon! Listening intently as the lady read the story, I tried hard to soak up every little detail and situation. When she was finished, we all waited backstage to take our turns. My turn came somewhere toward the end, so I had plenty of time to rehearse it in my mind. Hey, that blue ribbon was as good as mine! Over and over, I told the story back to myself, and when it came time for me to perform, I stepped out on the stage, full of confidence. Good grief! Where did all those people come from? I opened my mouth, and nothing came out. I cleared my throat and started over. To make a long story short…. I made a long story short! I told that story just as quickly as I could, leaving about half of it out, and quickly made my exit. Needless to say, there was no blue ribbon to hang in that spot on my wall.

Now, there is a story that I have no trouble at all in telling. It's the story of Jesus, it's the story of His love, it's the story of salvation.

"Blessed assurance, Jesus is mine! Oh, what a foretaste of glory divine! Heir of salvation, purchase of God, born of his spirit, washed in his blood. This is my story…"

54

Saddling Dan

I spent the first of many, many nights with Mary Shannon when I was in third grade. We were "best buds" from that time all the way through the sixth grade when she began attending school in Conroe. Mary lived in Dobbin, and it was an adventure just to get to her house. Her mom taught second grade at Magnolia Elementary, and when school was out on Friday, Mary and I would climb in the back seat of their car to begin our journey.

Our first stop was always at Alford's Café, where we would run inside and buy a coke and a package of potato chips to eat on the way to Mary's house. I still laugh today when I think of how Mrs. Shannon drove the car. She would hold the steering wheel with her elbows locked and her hands at the 9 o'clock and 3 o'clock-position and drive about 45 miles per hour all the way to Dobbin. I thought we'd NEVER get there!

The very first thing we would do when we got to Mary's house was run out to the pasture and catch her paint horse, Dan. After we caught him, we'd run inside and change clothes while "Grandpa" saddled him for us. Mary's grandfather lived with her, and he enjoyed sitting outside under the huge oak tree in his rocking chair. I called him Grandpa just like Mary did. He was a lot of fun and spent most of his time teasing us when he wasn't telling us stories. One Friday afternoon, however, Grandpa decided he wasn't going to saddle Dan for us. Settling back in his rocking chair, he told us we'd have to saddle him ourselves or ride bareback. I can still see him sitting there, rocking back and forth with a huge grin on his face as Mary and I struggled with that saddle. Keep in mind that I was very small for an eight-year-old, and Mary wasn't much bigger. We had no problem with the bridle, as Dan would hold his head down and let us put it on, but every time we'd try to hoist the saddle on his back, the blanket would slip off. Grandpa just kept on rocking and grinning.

Finally, I came up with a great idea. There was a large limb that hung low on the old oak tree, so I told Mary that I would climb the tree and she could hand the saddle up to me. Then she could lead Dan under the limb, and I would just drop the saddle on his back. Great idea! However, either she couldn't raise it high enough, or I couldn't reach low enough to make it work. Grandpa was no help at all…. he just kept rocking and grinning. What to do? Another great idea! "Run get the rope out of the barn," I told Mary. "We'll use it to get the saddle up in the tree." When she got back with the rope, Mary tossed one end up to me and I looped it over a limb while she tied the other end around the saddle horn. I noticed that Grandpa had stopped rocking and was watching intently. Mary grabbed the loose end, hoisted the saddle up to me, and I dropped it on his back. Voila! It worked like a charm! Grandpa just slapped his leg as he began rocking again. "You kids are something else!" he said with a laugh. I dropped down out of the tree, and we tightened the cinch by hanging onto the end of it while we lifted our feet off the ground. Whew! We were finally ready to have some fun. As we rode down the driveway, heading for unknown adventures, I turned and waved to Grandpa. I can still see him in my mind, rocking and waving under that huge oak tree, with a big smile on his face. I think he was proud of us, and that made me smile too.

Reflecting on that time, I find myself wondering how often I do things that cause God to smile. I think I need to get busy.

2 Corinthians 5:9 – "Therefore we also have as our ambition, whether at home or absent, to be pleasing to Him."

Me and Mary tap dancing at a Magnolia, TX Mardi Gras

55

Riding the Calf

I can clearly recall the first time I discovered that my pleasure might come at someone or something else's expense.

When I was around 10 or 11 years old, I was over at my friend Gaye's house, and we decided to go see what Marvin and Steve Dorris were up to. The Dorrises lived just across the street and down the road a little from Gaye. When we got there, Marvin and Steve were behind their house watching a young calf that was penned up in a small wooden corral. I think Mr. Dorris was probably weaning it because it was in there all by itself. The calf wasn't very old, probably around 5-6 months, and it was running around, jumping and bucking and just plain feeling good. We all stood there and watched it for several minutes, until someone mentioned that it would be fun to try to ride it. Well, it sure sounded like a plan to me!

Quickly, we climbed into the small corral and herded the calf up into a corner. Since Marvin was the oldest, it was decided that he would ride first. Steve, Gaye, and I grabbed on to the calf's head and shoulders while Marvin climbed aboard, but it wasn't long before he went flying. Of course, I had to go second, and I didn't last long either. What great fun this was! When it began to get tired, we would run up behind it and yell and wave our arms to make it jump some more. When I finally climbed aboard for my last ride, the calf just took a couple of hops and stood still. I kicked it a few times to try to get it to buck some more, but it didn't move. Sliding off its back I walked over to my friends, grumbling because it looked like our fun was over, and then I happened to look back at the calf. The poor little thing was standing with its front legs spread apart, head drooped close to the ground, sides heaving as it tried to get air into its lungs...and its tongue was hanging out. Quite a different picture from 30 minutes earlier when it had been frolicking happily around the corral.

As I stood there staring, my stomach felt like the calf had kicked it, and a huge lump came up in my throat as my eyes misted over. I felt horrible. What had been a fun and exciting time for my friends and me had caused nothing but fear and suffering for that poor little calf. I vowed right then to never mistreat another animal.

I'll never get that image out of my mind, but then maybe I'm not supposed to. It's a good reminder that I need to think about my actions and how they will affect others. All I need to do is follow a simple rule that God outlined for us in His Word:

Luke 6:31 – "And as ye would that men should do to you, do ye also to them likewise."

56

Saved!

In church one morning, we were blessed to observe the baptism of a young boy about eight or nine years old. He was grinning from ear to ear as he waited to be baptized, and the smile on his face when he came up out of the water lit up the entire church.

The scene took me back to the time when I was nine years old. My parents took Jimmy and me to Sunday School and church every Sunday, and we always read the Bible together as a family before going to bed at night. Ever since I can remember, Bible stories were read to me and I was taught about Jesus.

By the time I was around nine years old, I began to feel a little uncomfortable in church when the invitation was extended at the end of the worship service. I didn't really understand why, and I began to listen more closely to what Brother Gerald was saying about asking Jesus into our hearts. This resulted in several conversations with my parents, and finally I realized that the uncomfortable feeling was a tug on my heart from Jesus, asking me to accept Him as my Savior. Wow! I could hardly wait until the next Sunday so I could do that. But when the time came, I just couldn't make myself step out into that aisle and walk all the way up to the front of the church in front of all those people. We always sat on about the sixth or seventh row, and that was a LONG way to walk with everyone looking at you. Especially if you're only nine years old. So, I told my parents that the next Sunday I was going to sit by myself on the front row, and then all I'd have to do would be to just take two steps and I'd be right there with Brother Gerald.

Well… here came Sunday, and there I sat, and there I stayed. It was like my feet were glued to the floor. After church, Jimmy grinned and asked, "What happened? I thought you were going up today." I told him that I just couldn't move, I was too scared. Same thing happened the next Sunday and for a few Sundays after that, until I finally worked up the courage to take the big step. Well, actually two steps… and then Brother Gerald had me by the hand and everything was good! When he asked me if I wanted to ask Jesus into my heart. I think I almost shouted, "Yes!"

Then came another hurdle to overcome. I was going to be baptized in front of the whole church, in water that came up almost to my chin, and I couldn't swim. Now you might think that's silly, but to a little girl who was quite small for her age, it was a pretty scary thing. When the big moment came, though, Brother Gerald took me by the hand at the top of the steps leading into the baptistery, and he led me all the way out into the middle. I had a death grip on his hand, and he never turned me loose. I felt my fear go away as I stood there and listened to him say he was baptizing me in the name of the Father, and the Son, and the Holy Ghost. Then he gently laid me back under the water, raised me back up, and it was done! I'll forever remember how wonderful I felt, and I know my smile lit up the church too. I was now a child of God, and Jesus would be in my heart for ever and ever. Awesome!!

Looking back at that time, I can see how Brother Gerald's actions modeled God's. Both times that I was afraid, he took me by the hand and made everything okay. All I need to do is keep holding God's hand and everything will be just fine.

Isaiah 41:13 – "For I the Lord thy God will hold thy right hand, saying unto thee, Fear not; I will help thee."

57

My Name was on the List

One of the worst punishments I ever endured in elementary school was staying in at recess. I lived for recess. It was the highlight of my school day. Gosh…at recess you could run races, and yell as loud as you could, and get on your knees in the dirt and play marbles. You could go fast on the merry-go-round, swing way out on the johnny-strikes, walk across the top of the monkey bars, slide down the sliding board backwards, play football with the boys, wrestle with your friends. All kinds of fun things. So, you can see how tough it was for me one day in the fourth grade, when I experienced staying in at recess for the first time. And it wasn't even my fault. I guess you could say it was a slight misunderstanding. The misunderstanding part being that I thought I could get away with something just because a friend of mine was responsible for taking names that day.

Mrs. Byrne, our teacher, had to leave the room for a little while and she assigned someone in class to take names of the kids who misbehaved while she was gone. Now, whether that is right or wrong for a teacher to do, it was just the way things were done back then. Since the "name taker" was a friend of mine, I decided to have a little fun by making the ugliest faces I could at him, causing the other kids to laugh. Then, a wadded-up piece of paper just seemed to leap from my hand toward the waste basket. I used to love doing that. Throwing paper at the wastebasket. Oh, I had great fun. Soon Mrs. Byrne came back in class and took the piece of paper from my friend's hand and class began once again. When the bell rang for recess, I quickly got up from my desk to go outside with my friends. Then I heard her. "Tarvah," Mrs. Byrne said, "You will be staying in from recess today, and you will also wash down the blackboards while you stay inside." I didn't need to look at the faces of my classmates, because I could just feel all the grins that were aimed at me. Oh, this was humiliating as well as very disappointing. Not go to recess? Wash the blackboards? ME? Just because my name was on a piece of paper? Well, that was a hard-earned lesson for me, and I made sure that there was no way a teacher would ever see my name on a list like that again.

From that time on, I made every effort to keep my name from showing up on "the bad list," but I did make sure there was one list where my name would appear. I made a decision, early in life, that I wanted my name on God's list!

Luke 10:20 – "Nevertheless, do not rejoice in this, that the spirits are subject to you, but rejoice that your names are written in heaven."

Revelation 3:5 – "The one who conquers will be clothed thus in white garments, and I will never blot his name out of the book of life. I will confess his name before my Father and before his angels."

58

Joe Neal Allen

"Joe Neal Allen was a good boy." I know it's true. My teacher said so. I didn't know Joe Neal Allen… but I'll never forget him.

Back when I was in 4th grade, here in Magnolia, all twelve grades were housed on one campus. The gymnasium divided the campus into two parts, with the 1st through 6th grades on one side and 7th through 12th on the other. At certain times of the year, the high school boys moved the weights and benches outside behind the gym and lifted weights during their athletic classes. When we were outside on the playground behind our classrooms, we could see them working out and often watched them from a short distance away. They would strain and struggle, and they shouted encouragement to each other.

One day, we looked over and saw a bunch of boys just standing around in a huddle, and they were being very quiet. Before we could run over and see what was going on, the school bell rang, signaling the end of recess. We all went back inside to the classroom but our teacher, Mrs. Byrne, wasn't there so we began doing what kids always do when the teacher isn't in the room. I think we had more fun then than we did on the playground! Before too long, she came in and we could tell something was wrong. Instead of reprimanding us, she asked us to go to our desks and sit quietly as she had something bad to tell us. With tears in her eyes, she said that one of the high school boys had just died while he was lifting weights. What? Kids don't die. Only real old people die. At least that was how I viewed death as a nine-year-old. She then told us to get out our pencils and notebook paper, and to copy what she wrote on the blackboard. We were to write it 25 times. I can still see the words in my mind as she slowly wrote, "Joe Neal Allen was a good boy." Obediently, I filled up my paper with the words, writing very carefully. As it turned out, she knew him personally. She said she didn't want us to ever forget him, and I never have. The 1954 annual was dedicated to his memory. "Joe Neal Allen was a good boy." I know it's true. My teacher said so.

I have another Teacher now. I read His words every day and have committed many of them to memory. They have not only been imprinted in my mind, but also engraved on my heart.

John 11:25-26 says, "I am the resurrection and the life; he who believes in Me, though he die, yet shall he live, and whoever lives and believes in Me shall never die."

I know it's true. Jesus said so.

59

The Sugar Bowl

The little breakfast alcove in the kitchen of the home where I grew up holds a lot of memories for me and my family, but there's one incident in particular that stands out. It happened when I was in the third grade.

I was never much of a morning person, and my brother made the most of that situation. Jimmy loved to pick at me and get me all stirred up, probably because it was so easy for him to do. One morning we were getting ready to sit down for breakfast and he made a face at me behind Mom's back. Of course, being very vocal (even then) I very loudly shouted, "Stop it!" Mom gave us a look, but the "harassment" continued. He had this special way of just looking at me even without making a face, and of course, Mom never saw it. "Make him quit looking at me like that," I'd yell. "I'm not doing anything to her, Mom, I'm just sitting here," Jimmy would say. But I knew better. I KNEW what he was doing. "Just quit looking at him and you won't see anything," Mom would say. Well, of course I couldn't quit checking to see if he was still giving me "that look" and I'd say, "He's doing it again!" "Am not!" "Are too!" On, and on, and on. Finally, *the incident* happened… Mom slammed her fist down on the kitchen table and loudly stated, "That's enough!" Jimmy and I watched in horror as the glass sugar bowl bounced off the table and shattered on the tile floor, scattering glass and sugar everywhere. Total silence. Then Mom sat down, and we saw a tear roll down her face. We were devastated. Jimmy started picking up the pieces of glass and I got the broom and dustpan and started sweeping up the sugar. Mom had *never* acted like this. Gosh, what had we done to her? "We're sorry, Mom." "We won't ever do it anymore," we promised. I still remember feeling so bad that we had made her so upset at us and caused her to cry. After we got it all cleaned up, we sat down to a very quiet breakfast. I'll have to be honest and say that we broke our promise before too long, but we never pushed her quite that far again. It left such an imprint on our minds that even after we had become adults, we'd sometimes look at each other and say, … "Remember when Mom broke the sugar bowl?"

How many times do we do that same thing to God and grieve His Spirit? Don't you know He gets fed up with our constant feuding and bickering; our constant complaining and gossiping; our constant disobedience? Is it any wonder that sometimes God must "break our sugar bowl" to get our attention?

Ephesians 4:29-32 – "Do not let any unwholesome talk come out of your mouths, but only what is helpful for building others up according to their needs, that it may benefit those who listen. And do not grieve the Holy Spirit of God, with whom you were sealed for the day of redemption. Get rid of all bitterness, rage and anger, brawling and slander, along with every form of malice. Be kind and compassionate to one another, forgiving each other, just as in Christ, God forgave you."

60

Daddy Danced with the Indians

When I was about 10 years old, our family took a road trip to Colorado. One of my mom's ex-students and her husband owned a motel in Manitou Springs and she had invited us to visit and stay in the motel at no cost to us. It was too good of an offer to pass up, so when school was out for the summer we headed for Colorado.

I was very excited because at that time I was really into cowboys and Indians, and Daddy said there were Indians in Colorado. As we approached the foothills in Colorado, Daddy said, "Look at the top of those hills, Tarvah. Can't you just see the Indians lined up all along the skyline, sitting on their war ponies, ready to attack us?" And you know what? I could see those Indians! They had war bonnets on and held their lances high in the air as they yelled and shouted and looked down on us speeding along the highway below. I think I might have even shuddered. Jimmy would just roll his eyes, but I loved the way Daddy made the west come alive.

After we had been in Manitou Springs a day or so, Daddy made a big announcement. We were going to visit some cliff dwellings nearby, and some real Indians would be there! I could hardly wait to see them and didn't sleep much that night. Sure enough, as we approached the cliff dwellings, I could hear drums beating. Indians! As we got even closer, we could see them in their full regalia, dancing to the beat of the drums. Several tourists were sitting on large boulders around the dance area, so we quickly found some vacant ones and took our seats. I just sat there in awe, as I watched them shuffle around a huge fire chanting their songs. Then it happened. When the dance had finished and the Indians were gathered in a small group, I saw Daddy go over and begin to talk to them. Then, wonder of wonders, one of the Indians took off his war bonnet and handed it to Daddy, who proceeded to put it on his head. As the drums began to beat again, the Indians took their places and there went Daddy right out there with them. Around and around in the circle he went, chanting and shuffling his feet… the Indians in full regalia, and my dad in slacks, sport shirt, and war bonnet. The tourists began clapping, and I'm sure Jimmy, at 15, was totally mortified, but I thought it was just the grandest thing. Daddy, my hero, was dancing with the Indians!

That picture is forever imbedded in my mind, and it's one of my most cherished memories of him. He was always full of fun, and one of the things he used to say quite often was, "Let's go make a memory." Well, Daddy made a wonderful memory for me that day, and I'll cherish it forever. I was always proud that he was my dad.

I have another "Father" memory that I can cherish for all eternity. It's the memory of when I became a child of the Heavenly Father, and I'll always be thankful for His love.

John 1:12 – "But to all who did receive him, who believed in his name, he gave the right to become children of God."

1 John 3:1 – "How great is the love the Father has lavished on us that we should be called children of God!"

I don't know who enjoyed it more, Daddy or the Indian

61

Flipping Tarantulas

When I was growing up, I always looked forward to "going to Waco." That was a little catch phrase that was often heard around our house because that's where my grandparents, aunt, uncle, and cousins lived. "When are we going to Waco?" "Are we going to Waco soon?" "We aren't going to church this Sunday because we're going to Waco." Big Daddy and Big Mama lived in China Spring, but my aunt, uncle and cousins lived in Waco, and it was easier to say than "going to China Spring." My cousin, David, was about two years older than me, and we always found something interesting to do. I clearly remember one visit when I was about 10 years old. There was a large vacant lot next to my aunt and uncle's house, and unknown to me at that time there were some very interesting creatures who made it their home. On this particular trip, after all the hugs and greetings were over David and I headed outside. "I've got something to show you," he told me. Grabbing a bucket, he filled it up with water and told me to find a couple of small sticks. I couldn't figure out what in the world he was up to, but I soon found out! Over to the vacant lot we went, and David began to search the ground. Finally, he found what he was looking for and motioned for me to come over. There was a hole in the ground about the size of my thumb, and he began to pour water down the hole. "Get ready," he said. So, I got ready. I didn't know what for…. but I got ready. Suddenly a black, furry leg emerged from the hole, followed by another furry leg, followed by a huge, tarantula! I jumped back in fright, but David told me not to be afraid of them because these tarantulas weren't poisonous. Pushing his stick under the tarantula's belly just before it got completely out of the hole, he flipped it high into the air. Wow, I had never seen a flying tarantula before! We quickly moved to another nearby hole, and this time he let me do the flipping. This was great fun! Before long we had flipped several tarantulas into the air, and I began to look around me. It seemed like there were tarantulas everywhere, and I thought that maybe TOO much fun could be a bad thing. Besides…we were running out of water. Carefully we made our way out of the "tarantula colony" and safely watched them as they swarmed all over the vacant lot seeking their revenge. Oh, what a wonderful adventure it was!

Thinking about it now, I can see how I could have gotten into big trouble. I had trusted David completely and assumed that he knew what he was talking about. Of course, in this instance, he was right, and there was no harm done. But what if he had been wrong, and suddenly we had been surrounded by, and bitten by, huge, poisonous spiders? God warns us to not believe everything we hear, because false prophets are in the world today and they can make lies seem to be truth. We can get into a whole world of trouble if we don't test their words against God's word.

1 John 4:1 – "Beloved, do not believe every spirit, but test the spirits to see whether they are from God, for many false prophets have gone out into the world."

62

Angel in the Christmas Play

At Christmas time, one year when I was about 10 years old, I learned a big lesson in humility. Our Sunday School department at First Baptist Magnolia, was putting on a Christmas play, and I was chosen to be the angel. Oh, wow! How cool was that? I would be the one to announce the birth of Christ to the shepherds in the fields! I was told that I would hold a large flashlight and read the scripture verses from the Bible. Well, I'd show them. I'd do much better than that. I would memorize the scriptures and recite them without having to read them. Everyone in the audience would see how smart I was to be able to do this.

I studied and I practiced until I had everything down just right, spreading my arms wide as I made the important announcement. Then came the big night. We all assembled on the stage to get ready for the opening scene, and then the big bomb was dropped on me. I was given a huge flashlight and instructed to stand in the baptistry, turn on the flashlight, and say my part. The baptistry? I was supposed to stand down in the baptistery, turn on my flashlight and not even be seen? I was just a huge glow and a voice? Down into the baptistry I went with my flashlight and my deflated ego. I listened to the others as they said their parts and then my "big moment" came. I snapped my flashlight on and began to say the words. I still said them from memory, although no one knew it but me and God.

I learned a valuable lesson that night. It's not the people in this world we are supposed to impress, it's God. I can still remember the feeling I had when I started reciting the passage down in the baptistry that long-ago night. Without being full of pride, and without having to try to impress people, I was able to concentrate on the words I was saying. I was filled with awe as I spoke the most wonderful and most important words for all the world.

Luke 2:10-11 – "Fear not: for, behold, I bring you good tidings of great joy, which shall be to all people. For unto you is born this day in the city of David a Savior, which is Christ the Lord."

Proud to be an angel

63

Pete and the Buffing Machine

Back when I was about 10 or 11 years old, my mom was secretary to the superintendent of schools in Magnolia. During the summers, she would only work two or three days a week, and most of the time I went to work with her. However, I never stayed around the office. As soon as we got to the school, I would set off on my regular journey to find Pete. Pete Baker was the school custodian, and he never seemed to mind me hanging around while he worked.

There was never a dull moment with Pete, as he always had something interesting going on. On this particular day, he was buffing out the floors in the high school classrooms, so all I had to do to find him was follow the noise of the machine. I hadn't stood in the doorway long, before Pete looked up and saw me. Immediately turning off the buffer, he grinned at me and said, "Well, Tarvah. What are you up to?" Of course, the first thing I said to him was, "Wow, Pete! That looks like fun. Can I do it for a while?" Pete just laughed and said, "I don't think you could handle it Tarvah. It's not as easy as it looks." Now, keep in mind that I was only 10 years old, and probably didn't weigh 50 lbs. soaking wet. "Please, Pete? Just let me try!" I begged. Knowing that I wasn't going to leave him alone, Pete finally agreed to let me try. He patiently gave me instructions on how to guide the machine and how to control the speed, and then he turned it over to me. As I stepped up to the buffer, my eyes were barely above the handles, and I had to reach up a little to grab them. Away I went! From the very beginning, that buffer was totally in charge! With the throttle as high as it would go, that thing took off with a mind of its own, and all I could do was hang on for dear life. Bang! Into the wall it went. I over-corrected as I tried to steer it away from the wall and it quickly drug me to the center of the room. As I leaned to one side, the thing just drug me around in circles. Gripping the handles with all my might, trying to hang on, it seemed to gain speed and we went flying across the room hitting the wall on the other side. Of course, I had forgotten all the instructions Pete had given me, and that buffer slung me all over the room. I didn't have hold of that machine...it had hold of me! I remembered then that Pete had said that if it got to where I couldn't control it, just let go, so that's what I finally did. As I stood there glaring at it, Pete's laughter drowned out the roar of the buffer. I turned to look at him, and he was laughing so hard he was bent over with his hands on his knees, and I began to laugh too! Pete was right… it was more than I could handle!

Remembering that experience, I can relate it to things in my life that I need to let go of. Mistakes I made; sad and unhappy memories that drag me down; past sins that God has forgiven but that I keep allowing to make me feel heavy with guilt. Things I allow to control me and sling me around. What I need to do is just let go of them and give God full control!

Isaiah 43:18-19 – "Forget the former things; do not dwell on the past. See, I am doing a new thing! Now it springs up; do you not perceive it? I am making a way in the desert and streams in the wasteland."

Philippians 3:13-14 – "Brothers and sisters, I do not consider myself yet to have taken hold of it. But one thing I do: Forgetting what is behind and straining toward what is ahead, I press on toward the goal to win the prize for which God has called me heavenward in Christ Jesus."

Our boxer pups were a little easier to handle than that buffing machine!

64

The Good Deed Club

As we sang "Living for Jesus" in church one morning, we happened to sing a verse that I don't ever remember singing before and it triggered a long-forgotten memory. The third verse starts off like this: "Living for Jesus, wherever I am. Doing each duty in His holy name." The words reminded me of a time in my life when I didn't exactly do that.

One summer when I was about 10 or 11 years old, my out-of-town friend, Connie Key came to spend a week or two with her older sister who lived in Magnolia. I always enjoyed Connie's visits, and we spent a lot of time together just running around town, riding bikes, and playing at each other's houses. One afternoon we were trying to think of something new to do and I came up with a great idea. "I know," I said, "Let's start a club! We can call it the 'Good Deed Club' and in order to be a member you have to do at least one good thing for someone every day, and it has to be for free." Connie thought that was a great idea, and so the famous "Good Deed Club" sprang into life. As charter members, Connie and I set off to do our deeds. Our first efforts consisted of simple things done for my mom and for Connie's sister. We got a couple of strange looks from them as we happily took out trash, dusted a few rooms, and swept off a porch or two.

The next day, we set out on our bikes to see who else we could help. Our first stop was at Mrs. Morgan's little apartment. Mrs. Morgan was a little older lady who was a clerk at Mr. Yon's grocery store. She lived by herself, and we figured for sure she would have something for us to do. Giggling, and just a little nervous, we loudly knocked on her door. She was somewhat surprised to see us, but opened the door and asked us in. "We just wondered if there's anything you need us to do for you," I told her. "We'll be glad to help, and you don't need to pay us anything. It's for free!" She just smiled really big and then asked if we minded going to the store to pick up a few things she needed. Of course, we jumped on our bikes and raced to the store, glad to be doing a good deed for someone who wasn't even family. She was so happy that she gave us a big hug. I guess that's a kind of payment in itself, but we didn't consider it as such. Finished with our "good deed" for the day, we spent the rest of the time just hanging out and watching TV. This went on for a couple of days, with Mrs. Yon, and Auntie being two more recipients of our sacrificial actions.

On the fourth day, I asked my mom if she'd heard anything from Mrs. Morgan, or Auntie, or Mrs. Yon about what Connie and I had done for them. When she said she hadn't heard a thing, I began to get all pouty and a little angry. After all, we'd done a lot of good stuff for people, and we weren't getting any recognition or praise at all. When Connie came over, we discussed the situation and decided we were just going to disband the club. Since no one else had jumped at the idea and joined up, we were the only two members anyway so all we had to do was just quit. And so, we did.

I remember that I had a kind of funny feeling about it for a while, but before too long we were back to doing the everyday things kids do…. just having fun.

Now that I can look back with an adult's understanding, I recognize what was wrong. Speaking for myself, I was doing all this just to get praise and recognition; just to be bragged on. I've since learned that the best deeds are done for God's glory, not mine.

"Living for Jesus, wherever I am, doing each duty in His holy Name."

Colossians 3:23 – "And whatsoever ye do, do it heartily, as to the Lord, and not unto men."

65

Impetigo!

There weren't many traumatic times in my life, but I can definitely remember one time in particular. When I was about seven years old, I came home from school with some bumps on my face. They itched a lot, so naturally I scratched them, and throughout the course of the day every other place I had scratched broke out in bumps as well. At first my mom thought I had caught the measles, but the bumps weren't red like measles bumps, and I wasn't running any fever. We quickly got in the car and drove to Dr. Coker's office in Tomball, where I received my diagnosis. I had impetigo! Dr. Coker went on to explain to Mom that I had probably contracted it from one of my classmates at school, and that it was very contagious. He prescribed the medication that Mom needed to apply to the bumps and told her to be very careful when she doctored me so she wouldn't catch it too. No one in the family should touch me, and my sheets needed to be washed every day. I realized that this was not going to be a good time for me, but I felt even worse when we picked up the bottle of medicine that Mom would apply to my bumps, and I saw that it was purple! When we got home, the first thing I had to do was take a bath and scrub all the bumps. Then Mom doctored each one, and before long I was covered in purple spots! I don't think there were many places on my body that I hadn't scratched, and as a result I was almost one, huge, purple bump! Oh, this was awful! I'll never forget the look on my dad's face when he got home that day. I swear I remember him actually taking a step back before saying, "What in the world?" My mom quickly explained that I had impetigo, and that he couldn't give me a hug or touch me because he might catch it too. That was one of the hardest parts of this whole thing; no one could hug me and comfort me in my total distress. But the other hard part was almost as bad; the teasing I received from my "mature" older brother. Jimmy alternated from pointing at me, calling me names, and laughing at my purple polka dots, to recoiling from me in mock horror, saying, "Oh, no, it's the purple monster! Get away! Don't touch me!" I tell you, it was truly traumatic to this little seven-year-old. I remember that I felt like the lepers in the Bible that I'd learned about in Sunday School. Now I knew how they felt when people would point at them and yell, "Unclean!" However, even though my dad couldn't hug me, he quickly put a stop to Jimmy's antics and assured me that it would be over soon. He said that even though he and Mom couldn't hug me, they loved me very much and were going to take good care of me. The best part of it all was that I could stay home from school for a couple of days until I wasn't contagious anymore. When I was finally cleared up enough to go back to school, I discovered that although I wasn't being doctored any more, some of the purple stains were still slightly visible on my exposed skin. I had quite a lot of explaining to do to my friends!

Remembering how all the purple marks looked on my skin, I can also remember how good it felt to be finally "spot free," and a chorus of one of my favorite hymns comes to mind: "Sin had left a crimson stain. He washed it white as snow!"

66

The Ice Cream Man

From the time my cousin Marian and I were 10 or 11 years old until we were about 15, we spent two weeks together every summer. I would stay a week with her, and she'd come home with me for a week. Marian lived in the Heights, in Houston, and going to her house in the "big city" opened up a whole new world for this little country girl. Her mom, Clydine, would take us to the large movie theaters and to the huge, public, municipal swimming pools. She also took us to an air conditioned, indoor skating rink that actually had a concrete floor. All I had ever skated on were the traveling rinks in a tent with a wooden floor. And there were sidewalks in front of her house and throughout her neighborhood that you could skate on forever. Her "Nonna," who I called Aunt Lilliebelle (my grandfather's sister), would crawl into bed with us at night and tell us stories and we would all giggle late into the night. On Sunday, we would get dressed up and go to Berean Baptist Church. Talk about a huge church! Our little Baptist church in Magnolia, that on occasion could boast a high attendance of 79, could have fit in their balcony! There are so many memories of my visits with Marian, but my fondest memory was the discovery of the ice cream man. One afternoon we were playing out in her yard, and I heard these funny musical sounds off in the distance. "What's that?" I asked Marian. "Oh, that's the ice cream man," she said. "Let's go get some money so we can get some ice cream." Into the house we ran, got our nickels, and ran out to the curb. Sure enough, the music got louder and louder, and then around the corner it came. What a beautiful sight! A small, white, van with all kinds of ice cream painted on it turned the corner and came down our street, stopping right in front of us. Wow! I had never seen anything like it. A man bringing ice cream right to our front door! To a 10-year-old who loved fudgesicles more than anything in the world, this was heaven on earth! The next day I was ready and waiting by the curb, with my nickel clutched tightly in my fist. Then one afternoon, we were watching a scary movie in her living room and got really caught up in the story. The first thing I knew, I heard the music playing really loud. Grabbing our money, we raced to the front door and down the porch steps, but as we got to the sidewalk, we saw the back of the ice cream truck slowly turning the corner at the end of the block. We missed him! Oh, how could we have been so stupid? Getting my fudgesicle from the ice cream man had become the highlight of my day. You can be sure that I didn't miss him the rest of the week I was there!

Now there is another One I am waiting for; however, I don't need to be standing by the curb when Jesus comes. He will find me wherever I am!

Matthew 24:40-42; 44 – "Then shall two be in the field; the one shall be taken, and the other left. Two women shall be grinding at the mill; the one shall be taken, and the other left. Watch therefore: for ye know not what hour your Lord doth come… Therefore be ye also ready: for in such an hour as ye think not the Son of man cometh."

67

Tricks on Dan

My best friend when I was growing up, was Mary Shannon. She started school in Magnolia when we were in third grade, and from then until she moved away in seventh grade, we were inseparable. She lived in Dobbin, and almost every weekend either she would spend the night with me on Friday night or I would spend the night with her.

One Saturday, when we were about 10 or 11 years old, we were exploring in the room above her garage and discovered a tuxedo and top hat hidden away in an old trunk. Immediately we started trying it on, squabbling in a friendly way over who would wear what. Suddenly, an idea came into my mind. "Why don't we practice some tricks on Dan while we're wearing these clothes," I suggested to Mary. Dan was Mary's paint horse, and we were almost constantly on his back when I was at her house. Mary thought it would be great fun, and so we spent the whole morning doing crazy things on Dan, perfecting our stunts. Mary was wearing the tuxedo pants and the top hat, and I had on the coat with the long tails. When we got pretty good, Mary said, "Why don't we go over to Frank's and put on a show for him? We can charge him two candy bars for the performance…one for each of us." Frank Hoffart owned a small store across the street from Mary's house, and we hung out there a lot. Well, over to Frank's we went. When we approached him with our idea, he thought about it for a minute and then agreed, but said it had to be a really good performance for him to pay us that much! We went back outside where Dan was patiently waiting and began the show. I don't remember every trick we did, but I definitely remember the grand finale. Mary was riding in front, and I turned around so that I was riding backward behind her, facing Dan's tail. The plan was to gallop across in front of the store and I would reach over my head and pull the top hat off Mary's head and put it on mine. However, Frank had other ideas. When I got turned around backward, he stepped forward and slapped Dan on the hip. I could hear him laughing as Dan immediately took off for home! I was flouncing around grabbing for whatever I could hold on to and wound up lying on my stomach holding on to Dan's tail. The only reason I didn't fall off was because Mary was sitting on the long tails of my coat! Well, Frank might have thought he had seen the last of us, but he was wrong. After all, we had worked hard for our reward, and he owed us each a candy bar. Back to Frank's we went, and after a lot of good-natured haggling, he paid up. Let me tell you, that was one, hard-earned candy bar!

Reflecting on this silly little story and the "earned" candy bar, I think about a reward that was impossible to earn for myself. My eternal salvation was paid for and offered freely to me by the very own Son of God.

Ephesians 2:8-9 – "For by grace you have been saved through faith. And this is not your own doing; it is the gift of God, not a result of works, so that no one may boast."

68

Peewee Was in Charge

Looking back at my growing-up years, I can see how most of my misfortunes were brought about by bad choices. There's one particular time I have in mind when I was about 10 or 11 years old.

As was often the case when I was that age, I was visiting Gaye Yancey and we were trying to think of something to do. Marvin Dorris lived just down the road from Gaye, so we decided to go over to his house and see what he and his brother, Steve, were up to. At that time, Gaye had a Shetland pony named Peewee. He was a cute little palomino pony with a white star on his rump, and I loved to ride him. Never one to walk when I could ride, I suggested that we catch Peewee and ride him over to the Dorris's. He was easy to catch with a bucket of feed, so we were quickly ready to go.

As Gaye was leading him to the shed to get the saddle, I said, "Hey, we don't need to saddle him. Let's just ride him bareback." "Are you sure?" Gaye asked. "He's pretty fat, and we can stay on better with the saddle" "Naw… I can ride just as good without one," I told her. "Come on, let's just go!" We both climbed on Peewee's fat little back, with Gaye in the front and me behind her (very glad that I had her to hold on to) and began loping Peewee down the road to Marvin's house.

We were almost there when his two dogs rushed out of the yard and began running around Peewee, barking at the top of their little lungs. Well, Peewee decided he didn't want to go to the Dorris's house after all and spinning around on his back feet he headed for home at top speed with the dogs yipping at his heels. I frantically grabbed Gaye around her waist as I felt myself beginning to slide off Peewee's back. Not only was I going down…. but I was taking her with me! We were both wearing shorts, and our bare knees and elbows hit that blacktop with a vengeance. Now I prided myself on being pretty tough, but when I looked at my bloody knees and elbows with little pieces of gravel and dirt stuck in the wounds, and the pain started setting in, I began to cry. Gaye was just as bad off as I was, and I think I remember that she was crying too.

Anyway…there we were, at least 100 yards from her house, and no way to get home but to walk. How do you walk when your knees are so badly skinned that you can't bend your legs? You walk stiff legged. And let me tell you, 100 yards is a long way to walk stiff legged and in pain.

We finally made it to Gaye's house and her mom, Juanita, met us at the door. Taking us into the bathroom, she cleaned and doctored our wounds while asking us what had happened. After we told our story, Juanita asked Gaye why we hadn't put the saddle on Peewee. "We were in a hurry and didn't want to take the time," Gaye told her. "Well, I hope you both learned a lesson," she said. Yeah, we both learned a lesson all right. Gaye learned to not listen to me, and I learned that I rode better with a saddle!

As I recall that bad decision, it brings to mind a term I've heard all my life, "think before you speak." If I had thought about the consequences, we could face from being in a hurry, I'd have agreed with Gaye about using the saddle. Solomon had warned us!

Proverbs 13:3 – "Those who guard their lips preserve their lives, but those who speak rashly will come to ruin."

69
Racing in China Spring

Running races was my very favorite thing to do when I was growing up (except for riding horses). Any time a bunch of us got together, I would always say, "Wanta race?"

I remember one time when we went to China Spring to see my grandparents, and I was about 10 or 11 years old. They were having some kind of town picnic, and everyone was gathering at the town center to have some food, fun, and fellowship. My grandparents wanted to go, so we decided to go along. Well, as soon as the eating was over I immediately drifted away to find some other kids to hang around with. I was always doing that when we went around crowds. If there were any kids around, I'd get right there in the middle of them.

Well, this particular time I found about 8 or 10 kids standing around talking, and I walked up and said, "Hi, my name's Tarvah and I'm from Magnolia. Anybody want to race?" Then one of the boys who looked to be a little younger than me said, "I'll race you!" We quickly drew a starting line in the dirt, picked out a tree in the distance to run to, and as soon as one of the other kids counted to three, the race was on. I beat him to the tree, and we walked back to the others to see if there were any more challengers. Of course, there were, and I raced every boy and girl in that group. When I'd lose, some of the other kids would race while I'd rest up for another challenger. I always hated to lose but tried to be a good sport about it and usually wound up challenging the one who beat me to race again, and sometimes I would win.

Soon it began to get dark and as the grown-ups were preparing to leave, I said my goodbyes. I thought it was funny that some of the kids said, "Bye, Magnolia." My mom told me later that she could always tell where I was and what I was doing even though she couldn't see me. She said she could hear kids in the distance hollering, "Run Magnolia!" Hahaha! They had a hard time remembering my name, but they remembered where I was from. Hopefully, I represented my hometown in a good way!

Now I run a different kind of race and I have a new Finish Line, an eternal one. I need to pray daily to keep my eyes on the prize and not let anyone turn me aside. I also need to remember Who I represent! Father, help me to run well and run straight.

Hebrews 12:1-3 – "You were running well. Who hindered you from obeying the truth?"

1 Corinthians 9:24-25 – "Do you not know that in a race all the runners run, but only one gets the prize? Run in such a way as to get the prize. Everyone who competes in the games goes into strict training. They do it to get a crown that will not last; but we do it to get a crown that will last forever."

70

Learned to Swim

I had a life-changing experience down on Hurricane Creek when I was 11 years old. I learned how to swim. Now, that might not seem like much to most people, but to me it was everything. All my friends already knew how to swim, but when I went with them, I was always confined to the "shallow end." I couldn't swim, and it was pretty humiliating. My friends would hang around with me for a little while, but then all the fun would always migrate to the deep end of the pool, where the diving board was.

Then... one afternoon, I went home with my friend Tommye Hodge and my life changed forever. Tommye's cousins and her Uncle Archie were also visiting that day, and Uncle Archie took us all down to Hurricane Creek to swim. When he found out that I didn't know how, he said he'd teach me, but I'd have to trust him, and I'd have to do just what he said. First, he took me out about waist deep and told me to raise my hands high above my head, take a deep breath and hold it, and then lie down face first on top of the water. He said that if I did that, I would float. It took me several tries, but I finally got it. Then he told me to kick my feet while I was floating, and to my amazement my body moved forward. Finally, he told me to use my arms in a swimming motion, and off I went. I could swim! However, the biggest step was yet to come. So far, all my "swimming" had been done in shallow water, where I knew I was safe. Now, came the real test. He picked me up and carried me out into the deepest part of the swimming hole. He said he was going to turn me loose and I would have to swim to shore. This was big. No, this was huge. I was really nervous, but Uncle Archie told me again that I could trust him to take care of me; that all I had to do was follow his instructions. He turned me loose, and I immediately began to sink. Down I went, fighting the water for all I was worth. He quickly grabbed me, lifted me up, and told me to try again. After I found out that he would catch me for sure, I had a little more confidence. Carefully, he held me until I was floating, and then he turned me loose. Off I went. Swimming! All the way to the shore! All the other kids cheered, and Uncle Archie had a huge grin on his face. Wow! I could swim! No more being confined to the shallow water with the other little kids. Now I could jump off the diving board into the deep water. No longer would I miss out on all the fun. My life had changed forever.

Looking back on that eventful time in my life, I realize that I learned to swim by trusting Uncle Archie and obeying his instructions, and I can equate that experience to a song that I dearly love. The chorus goes like this:

"Trust and obey, for there's no other way, to be happy in Jesus, but to trust and obey." At age nine, I trusted Jesus, and obeyed His instruction to accept Him as my personal savior. *That's* when my life truly changed forever.

71

Corncob Pipes

It's not a good thing for kids to be bored. Especially kids with any kind of imagination. That's when not-so-good things happen. Back when I was about 10 or 11 years old, I spent a lot of time at my friend Gaye's house. We usually always had things to do, like riding horses, climbing on the hay bales in the barn, shooting bows and arrows, playing ball, fishing, and stuff like that.

One day we got bored, and we were sitting around trying to think of something exciting to do. That's when I spied the corncobs. Now normally, corncobs aren't such a bad thing to see, but I had just finished reading Tom Sawyer, so you can guess where this is leading. "Hey! Why don't we make us some corncob pipes?" I suggested. Naturally, Gaye thought it was a great idea, so we set about working on our project. We collected two great specimens and grabbed a handsaw from her dad's toolbox to cut them down to size. His boring tool came in handy for hollowing out the center for the tobacco and making an opening through the corncob for a stem. Now...where could we get the tobacco? It just so happened that Gaye's parents smoked, so a couple of cigarettes weren't too hard to come by. We shredded the cigarettes and packed our pipes, and then tried to think of what we'd use for a stem. Into the kitchen we went to find a straw, but there were none to be seen. Aha! Elbow macaroni! We searched through the package, looking for a couple that weren't curved too much, grabbed the kitchen matches, and ran back outside. The opening for the stem had to be enlarged so the macaroni would fit, then we climbed up in the branches of a sycamore tree to smoke our pipes. There was a slight problem in that the macaroni was pretty short, and the corncobs barely reached past our noses. That didn't stop us though because we were determined to make it work. It took a little while to get the pipes to draw, but we really worked hard at it and finally got them going. However, we hadn't counted on how short that macaroni really was, and our lips began to get a little hot. Then, I don't know where we got the most smoke…. up our noses, in our lungs, or in our eyes. We coughed, we cried, we choked….and we got sick. Talk about two miserable kids! Even trying to get down out of the tree was a major undertaking. It was hard to see with all the tears in our eyes, and not only were the branches moving, but so was the ground. We finally made it out behind the barn and found a place to lie down until the nausea and dizziness passed. We had found something exciting to do all right, but we also discovered that exciting isn't always fun. That day, I learned that sometimes we bring our worst miseries on ourselves. If we mess around with stuff we're not supposed to mess around with, the odds are really good that we'll pay the price. God made it a point to warn us about that in His Holy Word, and I've finally begun to start paying attention.

Psalm 7:15-16 – "He made a pit, and digged it, and is fallen into the ditch which he made. His mischief shall return upon his own head…"

72

Game of Tag

When I was 11 years old, my family went to Annapolis, Maryland, to watch my cousin, Lee Gayle, graduate from the Naval Academy. Lee had graduated from Magnolia High School and had received an appointment to the U.S. Naval Academy! What an exciting adventure that was, and I was so proud to have my cousin take part in that ceremony. He looked awesome in his Navy uniform! While we were there, we visited a couple that my mom and dad knew during the war. Vernon and Tessie had six kids and we all had a blast playing together. One of the new games they taught me was a strange type of tag. When you were tagged by whoever was "it," you had to hold on to the spot where he touched you while you were trying to tag someone else. When you tagged another person, you then became "free" and didn't have to hold on to that place on your body any more. It was a lot of fun, but they learned really fast that they didn't want to tag me! I had figured out that I could take a flying dive and tag someone on the foot, and that would just about be the end of the game. Not only was it awkward to move around while holding on to your foot, but other parts of the body would begin to ache and usually the tagged person would give up. Whoever had to hold on to their foot while trying to become free was always the "loser."

Life's a lot like that game of tag. How many times do I hold on to something that just brings me down? If I didn't learn anything else from that game, I learned that it's impossible to be really free when I'm handicapped by something that I won't let go of. Whether it's a grudge against someone, a worry that I hang on to, a fear that controls my thoughts, or maybe anxiety about something that I have no control over, I need to let go of it and give it to the Lord. Just let go and let God. I sure don't want to go through the rest of my life holding on to my foot!

Philippians 3:13-14 – "Brothers, I do not consider myself to have taken hold of it. But one thing I do: Forgetting what is behind and reaching forward to what is ahead, I pursue as my goal the prize promised by God's heavenly call in Christ Jesus."

I loved all sports, but tag was one of my favorites!

73

Put Your Little Foot

"Do 'Put Your Little Foot' for us, Miss Hattie!" I begged. "Yeah! Come on, Aunt Hattie. Please?" Diane echoed. Diane was Mr. and Mrs. T. H. Yon's niece, and she was visiting them from Houston.

It was the summer of our 12th year, and whenever Diane came to visit, we were practically inseparable. Mr. and Mrs. Yon lived in Magnolia, catty-corner across the street from where my mom still lives. They owned the entire block where Magnolia Elementary School now stands, and Mr. Yon's old horse, Silver, roamed freely in that pasture.

The day started that morning when Diane knocked on my door. "Want to hang around?" she asked, with a huge grin on her face. Well, of course I did. "Going to Mr. and Mrs. Yon's house," I shouted to Mom as we ran out the door. The minute we walked into the house we heard a voice. "You girls want to make some money?" Miss Hattie asked. (I always called Mrs. Yon, Miss Hattie.) Well, that sounded like a great idea, so we asked her what she had in mind. Her plan was that we would clean her house, and for payment we could keep whatever change we found lying around. She also promised us an extra treat when we finished if we did a good job. Miss Hattie would place spare change around in different places, and if we dusted and swept in all the right places, we'd find the money. There would be a dime and a couple of nickels under a doily on an end table, maybe a quarter behind some jars or bottles in the bathroom, and occasionally a 50-cent piece in a place where you wouldn't normally clean. If you moved a foot stool or swept under the bed, you might even pull out a dollar bill! Needless to say, Diane and I didn't miss many spots, and when we had finished, we each had a couple of dollars to spend at Yon's store later that afternoon.

Now, back to the beginning of my story. Rushing into the living room where Miss Hattie was sitting in her big, overstuffed chair, we asked her what our special treat would be. With a huge smile on her face, she said she would perform for us and asked us what we wanted her to do. As always... our request was for her to do "Put Your Little Foot." In great anticipation, Diane and I seated ourselves Indian style on the floor and watched her get ready. Miss Hattie was a little on the heavy-set side and she wore long, filmy, floor-length dresses that accentuated her tummy. On this particular day she wore a black one and she had little black slippers on her feet. First, she took out her teeth and placed them on the table beside her chair (because she knew it would make us laugh), then pulling her dress up a couple of inches and sticking her slippered foot out in front of her, she began to sing… "Put your little foot, put your little foot, put your little foot right there… take a step to the right…." Then she hopped to the right and that's as far as she got. Seeing her sing without her teeth was funny enough, but then she started to giggle, and her tummy began to bounce up and down. Oh, it was the funniest thing we had ever seen! Diane and I laughed so hard we fell over backward and couldn't even catch our breath. Miss Hattie said, "Wait…let me start over…," and off she'd go again. Oh, it was just too funny for words! We laughed until tears came out of our eyes and our stomachs began to cramp. Falling back into her chair, Miss Hattie laughed even harder than we did and that made everything even funnier. When we finally caught our breath and slowed down to a giggle or two, Miss Hattie said, "Okay…. now let's go get some ice cream." Well, she didn't have to say it twice. Diane and I beat her into the kitchen and had our bowls and spoons out before she could even get the ice cream from the freezer. As we sat around the table, we talked about Miss Hattie's "performance" and enjoyed another giggle or two. It was a perfect ending to a perfect day!

Whenever I feel a little down and out, memories such as this can restore my hurting soul. Solomon, in all his wisdom, told us as much in God's Word.

Proverbs 17:22 – "A joyful heart is good medicine…"

Me and Diane with my ducks, Dinker and Danker

74

Singing the old Hymns

One of my earliest memories was standing by Auntie in the Methodist Church at the age of five "singing along with the big people." I remember that I felt like I was just as important as they were, and I tried to stand tall while I sang. "There's a land that is fairer than day; and by faith we can see it afar. For my Father waits over the way, to prepare us a dwelling place there. In the sweet... by and by..." Wow. How awesome was that? Auntie loved that hymn, and we sang it at her funeral.

As I grew a little older and learned to read, my mom showed me how to follow along in the hymnal. It was a kinda strange at first and it took me a little while to catch on. You would sing the first line of a group of four, and then drop to the next group of four and sing the first line of that one. By the time you got to the third or fourth line I would tend to get lost and sing the wrong line, but I finally caught on. Again...just like the grownups...I would stand tall, hold my hymnal proudly, and sing. "I come to the garden alone, while the dew is still on the roses. And the voice I hear falling on my ear, the Son of God discloses." I walked down the aisle at church one Sunday morning when I was nine years old and gave my life to Jesus. "Just as I am without one plea, but that Thy blood was shed for me. And that Thou bid'st me come to Thee, Oh, Lamb of God, I come, I come." I remember being so scared during storms when the lightning would hit really close, and the thunder would make the house shake and the windows rattle. "In every high and stormy gale, my anchor holds within the veil. On Christ, the solid Rock, I stand; All other ground is sinking sand." There were some sad times in my young life. Papaw went to be with His Lord when I was in junior high, and I loved him so much. Then my precious Auntie joined him when I was only 18. Again, I found solace in the old hymns. "Are we weak and heavy-laden, cumbered with a load of care... In His arms He'll take and shield thee. Thou wilt find a solace there." Yes, I remember how the songs that were written so long ago touched my life then and still mean so much to me today. It makes me happy to know that there will be lots of singing in

Heaven, and I will try to stand tall as I proudly sing with the others! "When with the ransomed in glory, His face I at last shall see. 'Twill be my joy through the ages to sing of His love for me."

We're told in the Bible, that God will sing over us. I'll bet He has an awesome voice. I wonder what He'll sing to me.

Zephaniah 3:17 – "For the Lord your God is living among you. He is a mighty savior. He will take delight in you with gladness. With his love, he will calm all your fears. He will rejoice over you with joyful songs."

75

Parachuting from the Tree

When I was just a little kid, our yard was full of big old oak trees and I loved to climb them. There was one special oak that had a big curve in the trunk about eight feet off the ground with a huge limb right by the curve. I could sit with my legs hanging down the curved trunk, lean back against the limb, and read a book for hours at a time. If my mom couldn't find me anywhere else, all she had to do was go outside and look up in that tree.

One day when I was about seven or eight years old, I rolled up a couple of comic books, stuck them in the back pocket of my blue jeans, and climbed up in my tree. Now when you're a kid, you tend to believe everything you see and read in the comics, and when I saw Nancy and Sluggo having fun jumping out of trees with their homemade parachutes I decided to get in on all the fun. Scrambling down from the tree, I raced into the bathroom and got the biggest towel I could find for my parachute. Back outside, I couldn't climb the tree fast enough. This was going to be great fun! Situating myself on one of the lower branches, I carefully gathered two corners of the towel in each hand and jumped. Whop! I hit the ground hard and sat there trying to figure out what went wrong. Ahh.... I know....I just wasn't high enough in the tree. Back up I went, and this time I didn't stop until I got to my reading spot. Whop! Same result. What was I doing wrong? Did I need to go even higher? Was I holding my towel wrong? As I sat there, pondering the problem, I decided that I needed to climb just a little bit higher and maybe hold the towel by different corners. Ahh...THAT was it. Throwing the towel across my shoulder, I climbed to a huge limb that was about seven or eight feet off the ground and sat down to prepare my "parachute." Carefully putting the two corners that were furthest apart in each hand, I looked down. I remember thinking that it was an awfully long way to the ground, but heck, Sluggo had floated down like a leaf, so why couldn't I do it too? Extending my arms high above my head, I pushed off. Thud! Yep, this time it wasn't a "whop" it was a "thud!" I had landed on my side, and it hurt real bad. Every time I tried to take a breath, it not only hurt, but no air would come into my lungs. I couldn't even cry, thinking I was going to die! After lying there for a while with silent tears running down my cheeks, my lungs slowly began to fill with air and the pain eased up. I wasn't going to die after all! Soon I was able to get up and go look for my mom. She gave me a hug and told me that I shouldn't believe everything I see and read, that sometimes it can get me in big trouble.

As I grew up, I came to understand more clearly that books and newspapers were more than capable of containing lies. However, I also learned that there is one book that is truth itself, and I can trust everything that it says! The Bible!

Psalm 33:4 – "For the word of the Lord holds true, and we can trust everything he does."

Proverbs 30:5 – "Every word of God *is* pure: he *is* a shield unto them that put their trust in him."

76

Killed the State Bird of Texas

I first learned how to shoot a BB gun at the ripe old age of seven. Jimmy had a Red Ryder BB gun, and at 12 years old he was very proficient with it and considered himself an expert; thus, he decided to become my shooting coach. I practiced with it all the time, and when he got tired of cocking it for me, he showed me how to do it myself. I would put the muzzle of the bb gun on the ground and pull the lever out of the locked position and then use my foot to push it toward the ground to get it cocked. From that time on, I was able to practice by myself.

One day we were at Papaw's house, and I took the BB gun outside to shoot at targets. There were a lot of sparrows fluttering around in the pecan tree, and I thought it would be great fun to shoot toward them and make them fly. It never crossed my mind that I would actually hit one. Then I saw this big gray bird land on a branch and start singing. Carefully aiming the gun at the branch it was sitting on, I pulled the trigger. Plop! Down came the bird, landing in a heap at the foot of the tree. I slowly walked over and looked at it. It was just lying there, very, very still, and its eyelids were half closed over eyes that would never see again. I began to feel sick at my stomach. The least I could do now was give it a decent burial, so that's what I decided to do. Then Jimmy walked over, and as we stood there looking down at the dead bird, he said in true, big brother fashion, "Well, now you've done it. You've killed the state bird of Texas. They can put you in jail for that." What? I didn't know it was a mockingbird, and I didn't mean to kill it anyway. They didn't actually put kids in jail, did they? I looked all around to see if anyone else had seen what I had done, and then asked him to help me bury it. Not only because it was the decent thing to do, but also to get rid of the evidence! So that's what we did. We buried it right there under the tree. My guilty conscience ate away at me all the rest of the day, and all I did was sit around thinking about how that mockingbird had been so happy; singing and flying around, enjoying the day, and then, "pop," thanks to me, it would never sing again. It didn't help matters any to think that "they" might be coming to get me and put me in jail. Papaw noticed the strange way I was behaving and finally he sat me down and asked me what was wrong. I just blurted out the whole story and told him that I hadn't really meant to kill the bird, I just wanted to make it fly away. Papaw scolded me for aiming the gun at the bird in the first place. Then he said it was good that I was sorry for what I had done, and he told me to just never do it again.

I remember that I felt a lot better after talking to Papaw and thinking about the last words he said to me, I'm reminded of what Jesus told the woman at the well. He was always ready to forgive, but He had a command that went along with that forgiveness:

John 8:11b – "And Jesus said unto her, neither do I condemn thee: go, and sin no more."

77

Chased by Wild Hogs

When I was 12 years old, I spent a lot of Sunday afternoons at Tommye Hodge's house. Tommye and her family attended First Baptist Church in Magnolia, and I would go home with her after church, spend the afternoon, and come back with them to church on Sunday evening. One particular Sunday afternoon we were exploring in the woods behind her house, and I heard something crashing around in the bushes not too far away. It sounded like something huge, but then everything I ever heard in the woods sounded huge to me. In a trembling voice, I asked Tommye, "What was that?!" She just laughed and said, "Oh, it's probably just an old cow or something," and kept on walking.

Trying to be much braver than I really was, I plodded along with her but kept my eyes and ears wide open. I looked around for a tree to climb, but we were in an area that just had small saplings and lots of underbrush. Suddenly, we heard it again, but much closer this time, and accompanied by loud snorts and snuffles! Off we went, running as fast as we could go. This was real scary stuff. There was some kind of monster loose in these woods, and it was going to kill us! Then, from out of the underbrush came three gigantic black hogs! Now I say they were gigantic, but you have to remember, I was not only very small for my age, but I was also very scared. Well, those huge beasts had giant sized tusks protruding from their jaws and they were pointed right at us! Suddenly, right in front of us we saw a huge tree with limbs close enough to the ground for us to reach. Up into that tree we went, and just in time. Tommye and I broke off some smaller branches and threw them at the hogs, and we yelled and clapped our hands, but it only seemed to make them mad. To our dismay, they rooted around for a while and then decided they'd take a nap right at the foot of our tree. Oh, no… we were going to be late getting home and would be in big trouble for missing church! Finally, after what seemed like hours but was probably only about 30 minutes, the hogs got up and wandered away. Whew! Down from the tree we climbed and went racing for home. Tommye's dad just laughed and laughed when we told him what happened, but it wasn't funny to us at all. I'll tell you what… as far as I'm concerned, that big old tree saved our lives!

Now, when I'm in trouble, danger, or afraid, I have a safe place to run to for protection and comfort. God is faithful!

Psalm 18:2 – "The Lord is my rock, my fortress, and my savior; my God is my rock, in whom I find protection. He is my shield, the power that saves me, and my place of safety."

Proverbs 18:10 – "The name of the Lord is a strong fortress; the godly run to him and are safe."

78

Riding Pine Trees

If you were a kid growing up in the country, there's no way you could ever be bored. At least I couldn't. If you have half of an imagination, you can always find something to do.

One day when I was about 12 years old, I went to visit my friend Tommye Hodge. Tommye lived in a log house in a little settlement of homes about halfway to Plantersville. There was also a huge barn and a large, attached corral with lots of young pine trees growing along the outside of the corral fence. This particular afternoon, Tommye and I were just sitting around talking, when she asked me, "Have you ever ridden a pine tree?" She instantly had my attention, and I quickly asked, "How do you do that?" This sounded like a great adventure! "Come on, I'll show you," she said, as she began running toward the barn. "Wait for me!" I shouted and began running to catch up.

The first thing we needed was a long rope. This wasn't hard to find at all since her dad had several of them hanging around. We grabbed one and proceeded out to the corral fence where the pine trees were located. The first thing we had to do was find a pine tree that was just the right size. It had to be young enough to bend, but tall and strong enough give you a good ride. Next, someone had to climb the tree and tie a rope around the trunk as close to the top as you could get. "I'll do it!" I said, and quickly began shinnying up the tree. I was pretty good at that. I could climb just about anything I put my mind to. Up the tree I went with the rope in one hand, and when I got up pretty high, I quickly tied it around the trunk and slid back down. Then, with both of us pulling on the rope, we got the tree bent to where the top was even with the highest rail on the corral fence. Then we tied it down with a slip knot. Before Tommye could move, I quickly climbed the fence and straddled the tree near the rope. "Let 'er go!" I shouted. Tommye then pulled the slip knot and released the tree. "Whoosh!" Away went the top of the pine tree into the air with me hanging on for dear life. I couldn't help it… I yelled at the top of my lungs. This was one of the most fun things I had ever done! I slid down the tree and together we pulled it back down to the top rail of the corral for Tommye to take her turn. It wasn't long before the tree didn't have much spring to it, and it wouldn't straighten up anymore, but fortunately, there were several trees just the right size that were close at hand. Tommye and I spent all afternoon riding those pine trees and whooping and hollering at the top of our lungs.

There was only one drawback to the entire episode. If any of you have ever been around pine trees you know that they produce sap; and sap doesn't wash off very easily. Not only was it all over my hands and arms and face, but it was also all over my clothes. Thing is…hay and pine straw tend to stick to sap, and so does dirt. By the end of the day Tommye and I looked like little walking scarecrows! We were filthy, but oh, did we have fun! Well, the log home and outbuildings are gone now, but to this day when we go by that place on the way to Navasota, I look over where the barn and corral used to stand, and I swear I can see several crooked pine trees. Always brings a smile to my face.

As I think about those crooked pine trees, the old saying "as the twig is bent, so grows the tree" pops into my mind. God's word has some encouraging words similar to that.

Proverbs 22:6 – "Train up a child in the way he should go: and when he is old, he will not depart from it."

Tommye and me with three chicken snakes her dad had killed

79

Going off the High Dive

The summer before I turned thirteen, I experienced a huge turning point in my life. It was the first time I can remember intentionally facing a huge fear and asking God to help me overcome it.

Back then, Tomball High School had a swimming pool that they opened to the public for the summer, and I loved to go there. They had two diving boards; a low dive which was three feet high, and a high dive that was 10 feet high. One day my cousin Marian and her two younger brothers, Greg and Bubbie, were visiting and our parents took us to the Tomball pool for an afternoon of fun. I had always admired the kids who would do a cannonball off the high dive and promised myself that one day I would do that too. It looked like so much fun! Well, on this particular day I decided it was time. It really didn't look like it was all that much higher than the low dive, so I was sure it wouldn't be a problem.

Up the ladder I went, with Marian and the boys closely watching. When I got to the top I confidently walked out to the end of the board… and then I looked down. Whoa! Through that clear water, you could see all the way to the bottom of the pool and instead of looking down only 10 feet, I was now feeling like I was 20 feet in the air. My legs began to get weak, and my stomach felt like I had swallowed a bowling ball. I quickly looked to see if my cousins were watching and sure enough, they were smiling up at me in anticipation of "the big jump." Turning my eyes back to the bottom of the pool, I felt myself begin to shake inside. There was no way on earth that I was going to do this because I would surely die. Hey, I was just a little kid. At 12 years of age, I was only 4' 4" tall! Slowly, I turned around and walked back to the ladder and climbed back down, the other kids moving over so I could get past them as they were coming up. I tried not to look at them, but I couldn't keep from hearing their comments. "Where are you going?" "Hey, the board's up that way." When I got back to where Marian and the boys were waiting, I told them that I wasn't feeling too good, and that I would just do it another time.

For the next few weeks, all I could think of was getting up the courage to go off that high dive. Finally, toward the end of the summer I decided it was do or die. (There's that word again!) So once again I climbed the ladder. Once again when I reached the end of the board I looked down. Once again, I began to shake inside. But this time I asked God to help me do this and a thought came into my mind. I figured if I sat down, it would make the distance seem smaller, so that's what I did. I sat down on the end of the diving board, asked God to spare my life, and taking a huge breath I pushed myself off. Splash! I hit the water way before I had thought I would, and it was actually fun! Back up the ladder I went, and this time I jumped off. The next time I ran to the end and did my cannonball. I spent the rest of the summer having more fun than I'd ever had in my life in that swimming pool. All because God had helped me conquer my fear.

There are still many times that fear rears its ugly head in my life, but from past experience I have learned to trust that God will be there to help me through it.

Isaiah 41:13 – "For I am the Lord, your God, who takes hold of your right hand and says to you, Do not fear; I will help you."

Holding my nose… ready for the big jump!   *Marian*

80

Jumping Shorty

Horses have always played a huge role in my childhood. As I've mentioned before, I never had a horse of my own but most of my friends did. There's one particular horse that I remember well, as he belonged to a friend I spent a lot of time with when I was growing up. Gaye Yancey had a neat little horse named "Shorty." He wasn't very big, maybe about 13 or 14 hands, and Gaye and I spent many happy hours on Shorty's back.

One day when I was about 12 years old, we were in the pasture by her house trying to think of something to do. We got this idea to build a high-jump pit, so we got a couple of long boards and hammered some nails into each one, about six inches apart. Then we got a shovel and dug holes to set them in. After searching a long time for something to use as a bar, we finally saw a cane fishing pole standing against the wall of the garage. That would work just fine! We stood and admired our handiwork for a little while, and then began the competition.

After jumping several times apiece, we quickly began to get tired. "Hey, I've got an idea!" I told Gaye. "Why don't we take turns jumping Shorty over the bar?" Gaye thought that was a great idea too, so we ran to the corral to get Shorty. We were in such a hurry to get started that we didn't take time to saddle him. It would be much more fun bareback anyway. After a short discussion, we decided to start with the pole about 2' off the ground, and since he was Gaye's horse, she went first. There was just one problem. Shorty didn't seem to share our opinion of how much fun it would be. He'd just lope up to the bar and stop. "Here, let me try it," I said. Gaye boosted me up on his back, and I made a little circle and loped him toward the pit. Sure enough, just when he got up to the bar he put on the brakes. We both tried several times, but Shorty didn't want any part of our little game.

Getting a little hot in more ways than one, we tied him up and went inside to get a drink. Gaye's dad, Dick, was in the kitchen and he heard us griping about Shorty's stubbornness. "I think all he needs is some encouragement," he said with a little smile. "I'll just go out there and watch for a while and see if I can tell what you're doing wrong." Back outside we went, and I climbed up on Shorty's back. In a little while, Dick came over and positioned himself a few feet in front of the bar by the side of the pit. "Try it again, Tarvah," he told me, with that innocent little smile and one hand behind his back. Toward the bar we galloped, and just when we approached the bar Dick brought his hand from behind his back and raised a little switch high in the air. Whoosh! He brought that switch down on Shorty's rump, and Shorty cleared that bar like it wasn't even there. Well, we went up together, but we didn't come down together. Shorty's feet hit the ground way before I did, and when I finally landed it wasn't on my feet! I could hear Gaye and Dick roaring with laughter as I rolled on the ground. Shorty just stood there looking innocent, so I started laughing too as I got up and dusted myself off. Well, it took a little "encouragement" all right, but Shorty finally learned what he was supposed to do, and we spent a happy afternoon jumping him over the bar. We just had to get his attention first, and Dick knew just how to do it!

Looking back, I can see many times in my life where I needed some "encouragement" to do the right thing. Life would have been so much easier if I had just done things right the first time!

Jeremiah 7:23 – "But this command I gave them: 'Obey my voice, and I will be your God, and you shall be my people. And walk in all the way that I command you, that it may be well with you.'"

Luke 6:46 – "Why do you call me 'Lord, Lord,' and not do what I tell you?"

81

"At Calvary"

I was 12 years old, in seventh grade, sitting with several of my friends on the back row of Magnolia Baptist Church. That was the name of First Baptist Magnolia back then, and our pastor was Gerald Canon. He had baptized me three years earlier when I was only nine years old. Brother Gerald was very good looking, in his early 20s….and he was single. I think all the girls in the church had a crush on him. I know I did. I felt kinda guilty about that because I didn't know if you should feel that way about your pastor, but it sure caused me to pay attention to all his sermons!

That particular morning our little group of girls consisted of me, Pam Moseley, Melba Hosford, and Joyce Evans. As soon as Sunday School was over, we hurried into the church so we could sit on the back pew. We had to move quickly, or the high school kids would beat us to it. Anyway, as we began the singing part of the service, Mr. Jeter, who led the singing, decided to take song requests from the audience. I knew Brother Gerald's very favorite song was "At Calvary" because he had mentioned it before, and I had been paying attention. I never missed much of what he said. Proud of myself for remembering and wanting him to notice me, I quickly shot my hand up in the air. When Mr. Jeter pointed toward me, I loudly said, "Page 96," as I smiled toward Brother Gerald. I remember that he looked back at me and smiled too. (You can see how this memory is etched into my mind. I can even remember the page number after all this time.) Then, to my absolute mortification, I heard Brother Gerald say, with that smile still on his face, "You know that's my favorite song, Tarvah. Why don't you and your friends stand up and sing the first verse just for me?" WHAT? Did he know what he was asking? Sing by ourselves in front of all these people? We had a full house that morning, with at least 75 people there! I don't know how the others felt, but I just wanted to crawl into a hole somewhere. We looked at each other as we slowly began to turn red in the face, and then we stood up and began to sing. I guess you could call it singing. We mostly just kinda whispered the words as we looked at our feet.

It took forever, but we finally made it through that first verse and then everyone else stood up and joined in. I had never felt so embarrassed in all my life. Because I wanted to show off in front of Brother Gerald, I had gotten myself and my friends into a very embarrassing situation. Lesson learned! Keep quiet and don't' open your mouth! (Especially for the wrong reasons!)

Proverbs 30:32 – "If you play the fool and exalt yourself, or if you plan evil, clap your hand over your mouth!"

82

Learned to Drive a Tractor

Pete Baker taught me how to drive a tractor the summer after I finished 6th grade. Pete and his brother, Jake, were the custodians for Magnolia ISD. Actually, Pete was a carpenter, electrician, plumber, painter, and groundskeeper, all rolled into one. My mom was the superintendent's secretary, and during the summer she worked at the school three days a week.

One particular summer, I discovered how much fun it was to follow Pete around. Poor Pete. I pestered him all summer long to show me how to do whatever he was doing. "Whatcha going to do now, Pete?" "Can we paint something?" I was full of questions, but he was very patient. Then one day something quite wonderful happened. Pete pulled the school tractor out of the Ag barn and motioned me to climb up beside him. Of course, I begged him to let me steer, then that led to letting me shift the gears for him, and you can guess where it went from there. Finally, after I had learned to shift the gears properly, he sat on the fender beside me and let me drive all by myself. Carefully I shifted into first gear, popped the clutch, and almost threw Pete off the tractor! He just grabbed on and hollered, and we both laughed out loud.

He let me practice driving every day after that until I got really good at it. But that still wasn't enough for me. I just HAD to actually cut grass! After I had begged and begged, Pete finally gave in and showed me how to engage the blades, but he made me go very slow while he rode with me. I think the only reason he let me mow was because the tractor had a belly mower instead of a brush hog. My grandest moment came at the end of the summer when he let me mow the football field all by myself while he watched from the stands. I took extreme care to get every blade of grass so the field would look perfect. I wanted him to be proud of me, so I did my very best. I was pretty proud of myself too, but my biggest reward was seeing him grin as he said to me, "You did a great job!" Wow!

Now I try to concentrate on trying to make Someone else proud of me. I know I don't need to impress God because He loves me anyway just like I am, but just as the old hymn says… "Winning the smile of God, brings it's delight!"

Colossians 3:23 – "Whatever you do, do your work heartily, as for the Lord rather than for men."

83

Playing Marbles *For Keeps*

My first experience at "games of chance" came when I was in 4th grade. I enjoyed playing marbles, and when I went to school, I always had a pocket full of them. Seems like my hand was always in my pocket, rolling them around with my fingers, just enjoying the feel of them. I loved all my marbles, and I had some really pretty ones. One of my favorites was a clear red marble that you could see through, and I wished I had more like it.

At school during recess, my friends and I would play a marble game that required digging four holes in the ground; three of them in a straight line and the fourth one at a right angle to the last hole, all of them about 2 feet apart. Whoever made all the holes first could become a ranger and then hit the opponents' marble to "kill" them and win the game. I loved that game, and any other game you could play with marbles. I can't tell you how many pairs of blue jeans I wore the knees out of while playing with my marbles. But there was one game my mom told me not to play. It was called "for keeps" and it was kinda like gambling. The players would draw a large circle in the dirt, and each one would drop several marbles into the center. Then a shooter would take aim from the line around the edge and see if he could knock a marble out of the circle. You could keep the marbles that you knocked out, and you could continue shooting at the other marbles as long as your "shooter" stayed within the circle. If your shooter rolled out of the circle, you lost your turn. I decided to play the game by myself just for fun to see how good I was. That was my first mistake. I got to where I could make my shooter stop right where it hit the other marble, and I could knock all the marbles out of the circle without mine ever rolling out even once. I could "run the circle" so to speak. Wow…was I good!!

Then I had an idea. I decided I'd play for keeps just one time, and no one at home would really know about it. I could just imagine how full my pockets would be with all the marbles I'd win, and some of the kids had clear ones that I sure would like to have. When recess came, I eagerly joined in the game, but something went terribly wrong. Instead of winning the other kids' marbles, I lost every one of mine…. including my pretty red "clearie!" I felt just awful. Who would have thought that I'd lose? Now I only had my shooter left and rolling just one marble around in your pocket wasn't much fun. It was a hard lesson to learn, and I wished I had listened to my mom. When I got home, my conscience made me tell her what I'd done. She just looked at me and said, "Well, I think losing your marbles is punishment enough and I hope you learned something." I sure did! It wasn't worth the risk of losing the marbles I loved just to try to get more like them, and you can bet I didn't play that game anymore!

Luke 12:15 – "And He [Jesus] said to them, 'Take care, and be on your guard against all covetousness, for one's life does not consist in the abundance of his possessions.'"

84

Dinker and Danker

There's just something about baby ducks that's totally irresistible. Anyway, that's what I thought when I first saw the two that I would wind up taking home with me.

I was twelve years old and had gone to visit my friend Tommye Hodge. We were playing in the barn when out waddled a mother duck with at least a dozen babies following her. Instantly we each grabbed one and began to cuddle it. That's all it took. I just HAD to take a couple of them home with me. I named them Dinker and Danker (who knows why). We found a cardboard box to put them in, and when her mom took me home, I proudly carried the box inside to show the little ducks to my parents. "What in the world are you doing, Tarvah?" my mom exclaimed. "You know good and well that you can't keep those little ducks." You see…. we had two boxer dogs that simply annihilated cats, chickens, and anything else that happened to get in our yard. "It's not a problem, Mom," I told her. "All I have to do is show them to Ricky and Ginger and tell them not to hurt them. They'll listen to me." To prove my point, I went outside and carefully lifted one of the little ducks from the box. The two dogs quickly came running. I put the duck on the ground and grabbed Ricky by the jaws as Ginger stood there shaking with excitement. "NO, Ricky," I sternly told him. "Don't hurt the baby duck!" Then I placed Dinker against Ricky's side and petted him, telling him, "Good dog, Ricky!" Turning him loose, I did the same with Ginger. Finally, I took Danker out of the box and both ducks began to waddle off the porch. The dogs were right on their heels, with me right behind them, warning them of the consequences if they didn't do what I said. We walked around like that for a while, and then I went inside and looked out the window. It was a funny sight. The dogs were following those little ducks all around the front yard, panting and jumping around, but they didn't do anything to hurt them other than knock them over once in a while in their excitement.

Then one night, when the ducks were about half grown, my dad told me to turn on the front porch light and watch what happened. It was early summer, and before too long there were scads of June bugs all over the porch. Dinker and Danker immediately began running around pecking at the June bugs. I laughed at their antics for a while, and then went inside. Later I went to check on them before turning off the light, and to my horror they were flopping over on their sides and couldn't walk. They couldn't even get their chests up off the ground and were just pushing themselves across the porch with their feet. Standing right over them and occasionally pushing them with his nose, was Ricky! With tears in my eyes, I grabbed him by the back of his neck, and shoving his head down toward one of the ducks, I began to whip him with my hand. "Bad dog, Ricky!" I shouted. With impulsive anger and hysteria, I had jumped to the conclusion that he had finally lost his restraint and hurt the ducks. When Daddy heard all the commotion he came rushing outside. Quickly taking in the scene, he yelled, "Stop, Tarvah! The ducks are okay, and Ricky hasn't hurt them." Then he started laughing and told me what had really happened. Dinker and Danker, in their feverish gluttony, had eaten so many June bugs that their craws were overstuffed, and they couldn't even stand up. I felt so bad about whipping Ricky for something he hadn't done that my tears kept flowing, and as I put my arms around his neck, I felt his warm, wet tongue on my face. Dogs are just like that. They love you anyway. And they forgive you. A whole other sermon!

Well… Dinker and Danker grew up with those boxers and they all became great friends. They would sleep together, and even eat together. Those silly ducks loved dog food as much as they loved hen scratch! That night I learned a valuable lesson. Things are not always as they seem, and terrible mistakes can be made if you rush into judgment. I wish I could say that I learned to control my impulsiveness and my anger…. but I'm still a work in progress!

Proverbs 14:29 – "He who is slow to wrath has great understanding, but he who is impulsive exalts folly."

James 1:19-20 – "Wherefore, my beloved brethren, let every man be swift to hear, slow to speak, slow to wrath: For the wrath of man worketh not the righteousness of God."

Dinker, Danker, and Ricky

Me and Ricky

85

Pinto Beans

Man, I love pinto beans! I mean I can even drink a mug full of nothing but the juice! From the time I start cooking them until they're ready, I'm thinking about how good they're going to be when I pour them over my cornbread. However, there *is* one time in my life where they almost did me in.

My mom used to cook a big pot of pinto beans on Friday night so we could have them for lunch on Saturday. She never soaked them ahead of time, so they took a long time to cook. Anyway, on this particular Friday night those beans had been cooking for a couple of hours and I began to think about how good they would taste. Gosh, they smelled good! I remember bugging my mom about wanting to eat a bowl before I went to bed, and I can still hear her saying, "Tarvah, the beans aren't ready yet. You're going to have to wait until tomorrow." Well, the temptation was just too great, and before too long I snuck into the kitchen and dished up a small bowl of those delicious pinto beans. Eating them quickly, before I could get caught, I then rinsed out the bowl and headed off to bed. I'm sure you can guess what happened.

About midnight, those beans began "speaking" to me and I woke up with a bad case of stomach cramps. "Oh, no," I thought. "I should have listened to Mom and waited for those beans to get completely done!" No matter which way I turned, my stomach hurt. When I thought I got "relief" from the gas pains and would almost drift off to sleep, here they would come again. After a few rounds of that, I finally got Mom up and told her what was going on. She knew exactly what to do, and a good dose of Baby Percy took care of the problem. Back in the day, Baby Percy was a great cure-all for all things stomach related! However, Mom being Mom, she wouldn't let me go back to bed without a mild reprimand. "Tarvah…. if you'd just learn to wait instead of trying to rush into things, you'd save yourself a lot of grief!"

As an adult, I still struggle with this issue in my Christian life. Instead of waiting on God to accomplish things in His own time, I jump in and try to take care of the situation my way, often resulting in catastrophe. But God, in all His wisdom, has given us clear instruction in His Word. We are to wait for Him.

Isaiah 30:18 – "Therefore the Lord waits to be gracious to you, and therefore he exalts himself to show mercy to you. For the Lord is a God of justice; blessed are all those who wait for him."

Lamentations 3:25 – "The Lord is good to those who wait for him, to the soul who seeks him."

86

Red Rover

Back in elementary school, one of our favorite games to play at recess was "Red Rover."

We would divide into two teams and join hands, forming two lines facing each other about 30-40 feet apart. The team leader on one team would look at the other line and call, "Red Rover, Red Rover, let ___ come over!" If your name was called, you'd run as fast as you could toward the other line. If you broke through the arms of any two team members, you could choose someone to bring back with you as you went back to your own side. If you didn't break through, you became a member of the opposing team. Then the other side would get to call a member from the first team. This goes on and on until finally one team has all the members, or if recess is over, the team with the most members wins.

We quickly discovered that if we just held hands the other kid could break through easily and we would lose a team member, but if we interlocked our arms with our hands gripping each other's wrists, we were strong enough to gain another member for our team. In the same way, when we were chosen to run, we looked for the weakest link on the other side where the kids were just holding hands, and we could capture another member for our team. I would always pick a big kid to join hands with so that we'd be able to withstand the assault. There was one time I remember that we had called one of the strongest members from the other team to "come over" and he picked our link to try to break through. I saw him coming at us at full speed and I closed my eyes real tight and let go of my partner's wrist. I was scared it was going to hurt so I was willing to just let him through. However, my partner had a different idea, and he gripped my arm even harder. Victory! Even though I had given in to fear and let go, my partner didn't, and we caught the other team's strongest member!

Thinking back on that time, I reflect on how God will never let us go if we belong to Him. So many times, I am weak and want to just give up, but then I remember that He is strong, and He is holding my hand. When God is for us….

who can be against us?

Isaiah 41:13 – "For I hold you by your right hand--I, the LORD your God. And I say to you, 'Don't be afraid. I am here to help you.'"

Romans 8:31 – "What, then, shall we say in response to these things? If God is for us, who can be against us?"

87

Sick on Pizza

I love pizza, but my first experience with it left a lot to be desired. When my brother, Jimmy, was in high school, a lot of his friends used to come over to our house on weekends and just hang out.

One afternoon, Glenda Glasscock, one of Jimmy's friends, made plans to come over and cook homemade pizza pie for all the group. (Back in the day that's what we called it…pizza pie.) I remember I was about 11 or 12, and believe it or not, I had never eaten pizza. Well, Glenda mixed up the crust and rolled it out and began adding all the ingredients…. lots of cheese, tomato sauce, onions, pepperoni, etc. With all the kids helping with the chopping and shredding, the pizzas were ready for the oven in no time at all. I remember how good it smelled as it was baking, and I kept opening the oven door to check to see if it was ready. Glenda fussed at me and said it would never get done if I didn't quit opening the door and letting all the heat out.

By the time it was finally ready I was literally starving. When she had finished cutting the pizzas into slices, I made sure I was at the head of the line. Gosh…I never tasted anything so good! The crust was nice and crisp, and the other ingredients so hot and tasty with all that melted cheese and stuff. I just couldn't get enough. I think "devoured" was a pretty apt description of what I did to that pizza. My mom warned me that I better slow down and quit eating so much or I would make myself sick. What? How could anything this good make anyone sick? I honestly can't remember how many pieces I ate, but I can tell you this….it was at least one piece too many.

Later that evening my stomach began to feel queasy. "Mom," I hollered as I ran to the bathroom. (I always did that. She had to come hold my forehead when I threw up. Jimmy used to say I was such a baby.) Well, before long that pizza that had tasted so good going down didn't taste so good coming back up. Why hadn't I listened to my mom? I didn't want to even THINK about pizza anymore, much less eat it. Kneeling on the floor beside me, Mom placed a cool wet washcloth on my forehead as she said, "Tarvah, if you would just learn to listen to me, you could save yourself a lot of grief." I don't know how many times I heard that again as I was growing up. Seems like I always had to learn everything the hard way.

It's just the same in our Christian lives. All we need to do is heed God's instructions and we could save ourselves a lot of hard knocks.

Proverbs 19:20 – "Listen to advice and accept discipline, and at the end you will be counted among the wise."

88

Standing at the Band Banquet

When I was in 8th grade at Magnolia Junior High School, I was the shortest member of my class, standing at a towering 4 feet 7 inches. Back then, the 8th graders were allowed to play in the high school band, and I practiced hard to make sure I was one of the ones who qualified. You'll have to understand, there were only around 180 students in the junior high and high school combined, so if Magnolia High School wanted a band, they took what they could get. Well needless to say, when I got my uniform, it had to undergo quite a few alterations; especially in the length of the pants. How proud I was to wear that uniform with our school's name written on it. When we went to marching competitions, everyone would know what school I represented. During football games, at half-time the band would make formations on the field, and I was so small that unless I was in the front of the formation it looked like there was an empty spot, or someone was missing. But I was always in my place, in my little body, in my little uniform, standing proudly with all the bigger kids.

My brother, Jimmy, was a senior that year and he played on the football team. I was so glad to be able to play in the band at the same time he was playing on the field. It was a fun year! Since there were so few student athletes and band members, our banquet was held together at the end of football season, and it was called the Football/Band Banquet. For the first, and only, time Jimmy and I would be attending the same banquet and I could hardly wait. To make it even more special…I had a date! Cecil Johnson was in my class, and he was also a member of the band. It didn't matter that I was so short because Cecil wasn't much taller than I was at that point in his life.

Finally, the big night arrived, and all my family went to the banquet. My mom was secretary to the superintendent at that time, so she and my dad were there too. There were no assigned seats, and band members and football players just intermingled throughout the cafeteria. I thought it was so awesome that I wasn't sitting very far from where Jimmy and his date were sitting. Soon after the meal was over, the time came for the athletes and band members to be acknowledged.

The football team was asked to stand first, and then it came time for the band to be recognized. The principal asked all the band members to stand, and I arose from my seat along with the others. There was just a slight pause before everyone began clapping, and during that pause I heard Jimmy say, "Tarvah, he said to stand up." Well…I WAS standing up! I'll never forget that moment as long as I live. I looked over at him, and he winked and laughed, so I laughed too, along with everyone else! I still smile when I think about that time.

Looking back, I remember that I was happy to be a representative of the MHS band, and I was proud to wear my uniform. Maybe everyone couldn't see me all the time, but those closest around me knew I was always standing in my place. Now, I'm happy to be a representative of God's family, and every day I try to remember to put on my uniform!

Ephesians 6:13 – "Therefore take up the whole armor of God, that you may be able to withstand in the evil day, and having done all, to stand."

I had a date with Cecil Johnson!

89
Afraid of the Dark

Like most other kids, I was afraid of the dark when I was growing up. It wasn't so much the dark…but what could be IN the dark, lurking in every corner, or in my closet, or under my bed.

For many years, every summer I would spend a week in Houston with my cousin, Marian, and then she'd come home with me for a week. We watched every scary show that would come on TV and begged to be taken to the movies to watch even more. I don't think we missed a horror show that ever came out. The Godzilla movies weren't so bad, but Creature from the Black Lagoon, The Creature Walks Among Us, I Was a Teenage Werewolf, Invasion of the Body Snatchers, The Blob, etc. were really scary. We watched and shivered through them all. It was great fun…until it got dark. It wasn't so bad going to bed at night while Marian was with me, but when she went back home, I was very careful to make sure my nightlight never burned out!

There was one particular night that I remember very well when I was about 12 years old. I had been over at a friend's house and when her parents brought me home it was already dark. The problem was the house was dark too. And empty. And unlocked. (We never felt a need to lock our doors back then.) I knew that my mom and dad were visiting Mr. and Mrs. Barbee, and evidently, they hadn't gotten home yet. I assured my friend's mom that it was okay to leave me because I would just call my parents and let them know I was home, and they'd be right there. The Barbees just lived a few blocks away. Well, as they drove off it seemed that the house just got darker and emptier. I cautiously opened the front door, flipped on the hall light, and raced to the phone. When Mrs. Barbee answered, I told her to please tell my parents I was at home, then, hanging up the phone I ran back to the front door because I had a plan in mind. It always pays to have a plan. My already overactive imagination was running wild. Maybe there was someone hiding in the house, getting ready to grab me. But then maybe he was lurking outside, around the corner of the house. With my heart pounding and my stomach quivering, I decided to stand at the front door and hold it half-way open so that I could run either way. If he came at me from inside the house, I would run away; but if he came at me from outside, I would run inside and lock the door. So, there I stood, with my body half inside and half outside, straining hard to see the glow of headlights coming from the direction of the Barbee's house.

When my parents drove up, I quickly stepped inside and shut the door. I didn't want them to know that I had been scared, but I SURE didn't want Jimmy to know because it was important to me that he would think I was brave. I could never let him think I was a "scaredy cat!"

What a wonderful assurance I have now, that I don't need to be afraid of the dark, what's in the dark, or even what's in broad daylight. I have God's promise that He will always be with me and will help me face whatever comes my way.

Psalm 91:4-6 – "He will cover you with his feathers, and under his wings you will find refuge; his faithfulness will be your shield and rampart. You will not fear the terror of night, nor the arrow that flies by day, nor the pestilence that stalks in the darkness, nor the plague that destroys at midday."

90
Killed the Mouse

The day started off like any other. Little did I know that before it was over, I'd become a 12-year-old killer.

I had spent the night with my friend, Gaye Yancey, and we woke up to the wonderful smell of bacon and pancakes being prepared in the kitchen. Gaye's mom, Juanita, always fed us well! Jumping out of bed we quickly got dressed, eager to start a day of fun and adventure. By early that afternoon we had already accomplished much of that goal. The day had been spent riding Shorty, Gaye's horse, climbing and jumping on the hay bales in the barn, and playing cowboys and Indians. Later that afternoon, as we put the bridle and saddle away in the storage shed where they also kept their horse feed, I saw something scamper across the floor. "What was that?" I asked. "Oh, that was just a mouse." Gaye replied. "They get in here all the time and eat the horse feed." "There's another one!" I shouted. "It just ran behind that sack of feed."

Now there were several sacks of feed in the shed, but there was one that immediately caught my eye. It was a sack of horse roughage chunks that had already been opened, and those chunks were just the right size for throwing. "Hey, I know what we can do," I said with a huge grin on my face, "Let's use these to throw at the mice!" Immediately we began creeping around the shed with handfuls of the chunks, rattling feed sacks to try to get the mice to run out in the open. "Wham!" "Bam!" It sounded like a war zone from all the chunks hitting the floor and walls. Mice were running all over the place, and we were hollering and jumping in the air to get away from them while at the same time hurling our missiles. Oh, it was great fun! Then, I actually hit one. Letting go with one of my hardest throws, I saw it hit the mouse and knock it up against the wall. Rolling over onto it's back, the little mouse just lay there with all four tiny legs quivering in the air. "Wow! You got one!" shouted Gaye. Oh, no. It wasn't supposed to happen this way. I just wanted to have fun throwing chunks of feed at the mice as they ran around. I never actually thought I'd hit one. I was always very tender-hearted toward animals due to the type of books I always read—most of them from the point of view of the rabbits, dogs, horses, and other animals. So naturally, I began to think of this little mouse enjoying its life here in the feed shed, running and playing and eating its fill, until I came along and put an end to everything.

Tears began to form in my eyes as I looked down at the little mouse, whose legs had finally stopped quivering. Just a few seconds earlier it had been so full of life, and now, thanks to me, that was all over. It was dead, and I had been the one who killed it. "Is it dead?" I heard Gaye ask. All I could do was nod because there was a lump in my throat. Without saying another word, we just put down the chunks and walked out of the shed. When we got in the house, I called my mom to come pick me up. While we waited for her, Gaye and I tried to act like we were still excited about our day, but the atmosphere had changed somewhat. It was truly a sad end to what had promised to be a wonderful day. I'll never get the image of that little mouse out of my mind, lying there slowly dying, just because I wanted to have fun. I found out that my feelings of pleasure could quickly become feelings of regret. God's Word warns us about such things. How different would my life be if I just paid more attention?

Galatians 6:7-8 – "Do not be deceived: God cannot be mocked. A man reaps what he sows. The one who sows to please his sinful nature, from that nature will reap destruction; the one who sows to please the Spirit, from the Spirit will reap eternal life."

Gaye Yancey and me (the killer)

91

First Night Away from Home

I well remember the first night I spent away from home…without any of my family members, that is.

When I was in third grader Mary Shannon enrolled in our class at Magnolia Elementary School and quickly became my very best friend. Mary was a tomboy just like me, and we enjoyed the rough-and-tumble games of wrestling, football, and Red Rover. She also had a horse. That was important because I loved horses!

Before too long, just hanging around together at school didn't give us enough time together, so I asked my mom if Mary could come home with me after school on Friday and spend the night. Of course, she said okay so we quickly made our plans. What fun we had, playing all afternoon, and then talking and giggling all night. Saturday came way too quickly, and we had to take Mary home. The next weekend, Mary asked if I could come spend the night at her house, and so Friday after school, we got in the back seat of Mrs. Shannon's car and headed to Dobbin.

We spent the afternoon riding her horse, Dan, and playing cowboys and Indians. I never had so much fun! After supper, we watched wrestling on TV and even tried out some of the holds we saw Danny McShane and Whisker Savage use on each other! Then….it was time to go to bed. We talked and giggled a while and then Mary went to sleep. But I wasn't sleepy, and that's when everything started going south. I just lay there and began to wonder what Mom and Daddy and Jimmy were doing. Then I began to feel queasy, and I felt this huge lump form in my throat. I rolled over on my stomach to see if that would help, but it didn't. "Gosh, I wish Mom was here," I thought. Closing my eyes, I tried to picture her face…and then Daddy's face. That just made things worse! Rolling back over onto my back, I squeezed my eyes shut and something wet came out of the corners. What a big baby I was! Then the lump in my throat got even bigger and I couldn't swallow. Something bad was going to happen and I was going to choke to death!

I quickly woke Mary up and told her to call her mother, and when Mrs. Shannon came in, I blurted out, "Mrs. Shannon, I feel like something's in my throat and I can't swallow!" She told me to sit up and open my mouth real wide so she could look down my throat, but of course there was nothing for her to see. She got me a glass of water, and after taking a couple of swallows I told her I felt better. Back to bed she went, but as soon as she turned out the light in our room, I started feeling sick again. Mary wasn't a lot of help. She just turned over and went to sleep. I felt sicker. Shaking Mary on the shoulder, I again asked her to call her mother. "I don't feel so good," I told Mrs. Shannon when she turned the light back on, "I think I'm going to throw up." By then, I think she had figured it out. "You're just homesick, Tarvah, and if you close your eyes and think about the things you and Mary did today, you'll go to sleep before you know it." Well, that's what I did, and it worked. When Saturday morning came, I was ready to ride Dan again and get back to the business of having fun. That was just the start of many adventure-filled weekends that Mary and I spent together, and I never again felt homesick. But I'll have to say, that first Saturday I was really glad to see Mom's face when she came to pick me up, and my home never looked so good!

Now that I'm older… there's another Place I'm getting kind of homesick for, and another Face I can't wait to see.

"What a day that will be when my Jesus I shall see,
And I look upon his face, the One who saved me by his grace.
When he takes me by the hand, and leads me through the Promised Land,
What a day, glorious day that will be."

Me and Mary Shannon

92

Mrs. Colburn's Punishment

"It's not fair!" I can't number the times that those words have come out of my mouth, but I do recall a time that it really wasn't, and the circumstances were a little bit painful.

It happened when I was in junior high, either 7th or 8th grade, I can't remember which, but I do remember it was in English class. Mrs. Colburn was our teacher. She had had polio when she was young, and she had a crippled arm and walked with a limp. She was also very strict, and I don't think she liked me very much. I can't understand why, but it seemed like she picked on me a lot. Couldn't have been because I sometimes whispered, or giggled, or passed notes…. nothing like that. Maybe it was because I was Jimmy's little sister. You see, back then the junior high classes were in the same building as the high school classes, and we had many of the same teachers. Mrs. Colburn was Jimmy's English teacher too. That must have been it! But no, I guess it wasn't, because I think Mrs. Colburn liked Jimmy.

Anyway, we were in class and one of my friends had whispered something to me. (I'm pretty sure it was Pam Moseley!) I just kept doing my work and she whispered again, a little louder this time. It was probably the only time in my life that I didn't whisper back, but I was the one who paid the price. Mrs. Colburn had been patrolling the aisles while we did our work, and suddenly I felt her hand on the back of my neck. She slowly gripped a few of the "short hairs" right at the bottom of my hairline on the back of my neck and began to pull. Well…if you've ever had those hairs pulled, you'll understand what I did next. There can be NO resistance! Letting out a little yelp, I jumped to my feet and tiptoed beside her, trying to lessen the pressure on my hair as she limped to the front of the classroom. "You're going to learn some day that you can't whisper in class," she told me. "But it wasn't me," I answered, as she headed toward the classroom door. "This isn't fair!"

However, my words were in vain as she propelled me through the door with her fingers still pulling my hair. "You're going to stand right here in the hall for the rest of the period!" Back then, if you misbehaved you were sent to stand in the hall for everyone to see, and if the principal happened by, you sometimes got a swat. Here I was, standing out in the hall, being punished for something I didn't even do. I remember that I stood there rubbing the back of my neck and feeling very nervous about who might see me. It just so happened that my mom, who was the superintendent's secretary, had her office in that same building and I just knew she'd come wandering down the hall while I was standing out there.

Well, she didn't and neither did the principal, and the bell finally rang signaling the end of the period. My friends couldn't wait to tease me, and since my neck had finally stopped hurting, I was able to laugh along with them. I'm sure it had been a very funny sight…me walking on my tiptoes as Mrs. Colburn limped along by my side, leading me like a puppy on a chain. It might have been funny…. but it sure wasn't fair!

I still remember that day with a sense of injustice, but that memory brings to mind another time in history when a punishment wasn't fair. A time that I will be "eternally" thankful for. A time when a sinless Jesus paid the price for the sins of the world.

2 Corinthians 5:21 – "For God made Christ, who never sinned, to be the offering for our sin, so that we could be made right with God through Christ."

93

Daddy Loved to Dance

Daddy loved to dance. He was really good at it, too. He could do everything from the two-step to the Charleston, to the waltz, to the jitterbug, and he taught me how to dance at an early age.

I loved to dance with my dad at any time, but there's one very special memory he gave me. When I was in 7th grade and Jimmy was a junior in high school, my parents let him have a party at our house. We cleaned out the garage and sprinkled soap powder on the concrete floor. For a "romantic" touch, Daddy put a blue light bulb in the overhead socket. Music was supplied by a portable turntable that was placed on the lid of the chest freezer that sat in the front corner of the garage. We had lots of records, and his friends also brought their favorites. If any of you have older brothers, you can identify with the crushes I had on Jimmy's friends. He had so many good-looking buddies!

I could hardly wait for the night of the party when I could dance with some of them. Keep in mind I was only 12 years old and not very "mature" for my age, but I had high hopes. Finally, the big night arrived, but it sure didn't start out like I had dreamed it would. I wound up just standing around watching everyone dancing and having a good time. After an hour or so, there was a slight intermission to give everyone time to eat.

Little did I know that Daddy had noticed that I hadn't danced with anyone. Suddenly, while everyone else was standing around eating, Daddy went over to the record player and put on a fast song. Walking over to me, he said, "Come on, Tarvah. Let's show them how it's done." Wow, did we ever show them how to jitterbug! I can remember all the older kids grinning as they watched us, and when the dancing began again there weren't very many dances that I missed. Daddy had noticed that I was really disappointed, and he knew just what to do. He'd always been my hero, but that night he was also my rescuer. Thanks, Daddy, for taking care of your little girl.

Reflecting on that time, I realize that I could always count on my daddy to be there when I needed him, and that he understood what I needed without me even telling him. That's what God does. He knows what I need and He's always there for me!

Isaiah 41:13 – For I, the Lord your God, hold your right hand; it is I who say to you, "Fear not, I am the one who helps you."

94
Fox Hunting

Growing up in the country was a wonderful childhood experience for me and my friends. There was never a shortage of things to do, and the woods and creek bottoms offered a variety of adventures.

One of those adventures happened to me when I was about 12 or 13 years old. I had gone home with my friend, Melba Hosford, to spend the night, and her daddy, "Britches" had promised to take us fox hunting. I could hardly wait for dark to come, because that's when you hunt foxes down here in the south. At night. Deep in the woods. When it's really dark.

Right after supper, Britches loaded up his hounds in a flat-top trailer and Melba and I threw our blankets and pillows on top because that's where we would be sleeping. Then we all got in his truck and followed a rugged, two-rut road deep into Lake Creek Bottom. When we finally got to where he wanted to go, he unloaded the dogs and built a small campfire for us to sit around while the dogs were hunting.

Since it wasn't quite dark, Melba and I explored the general area to see what we could discover, and then I saw it. A bear! Right there at the edge of the woods and looking right at me! I shouted and pointed it out, but for some reason it wasn't visible to anyone but me. When it ran off, I quickly said, "Come on! Let's go over there and we'll see its tracks and I'll prove it was there!" And there they were, crossing the road as plain as could be. I pointed them out to Melba, and she scornfully said, "Those aren't bear tracks," as she rolled her eyes. So... I hollered for Britches to come see. When he got there, he looked at the tracks and shook his head, saying, "Hmmm.... could be," and then he just smiled. But there was no doubt in my mind. I had spotted a bear and there were its tracks! Well...I know what I saw. (Or at least I was PRETTY sure.)

Back at the campfire, we ate some snacks and Britches told us stories. Wonderful stories. Stories of panthers, and BEARS, and things unknown that ran loose in the woods. We sat around for a long time listening to the scary stories, and sometimes Britches would stop talking and we would just listen to the hounds, baying out in the woods. Soon our eyes began to get heavy, and we climbed up on the top of the trailer to bed down. The next thing I remember was waking up as the trailer bounced along the rutted road. Melba and I hung on to the rails for dear life as Britches tried to get closer to the hounds. We got pretty close to where they were running, but never saw the fox.

Eventually Britches blew his cow horn and called the dogs in, loaded them up in the trailer, and we headed for home. I found out later that the fun of fox hunting was just sitting out in the woods around a campfire with your friends, eating and telling stories, and listening to the hounds baying. Britches said the sound of the dogs was like music to his ears! I was amazed that the dogs didn't get lost because they ran so far off into the woods that sometimes you could hardly hear them. Britches told me that all he had to do was blow his horn and they would come to where he was. He would blow it continually until every last dog came in.

Jesus is like that. No matter how far away from Him we get He continues to call us back. We just need to listen.

John 10: 27 – "My sheep hear My voice, and I know them, and they follow Me."

Melba Hosford

95
Mr. Yon's Store

Walmart doesn't have a thing on T. H. Yon General Merchandise. Back when I was growing up in the early 50s, Yon's store was the "one stop shopping center" for Magnolia. You could purchase anything from groceries, to pots and pans, clothes, shoes, and hats. There was also a huge room in the back of the store that held 50lb sacks of feed, grain, flour, corn meal, etc., and directly behind the meat market, was an attached icehouse that contained huge blocks of ice. Looking back on that time, I can see where my friend Diane and I could have gotten in real big trouble. Diane was Mr. Yon's niece, and when she visited from Houston sometimes the store became our playground. It was great fun to climb on the feed sacks in the back. If you were lucky, the sacks would be unevenly stacked and staggered so you could jump from one stack to the other and get all the way up to the ceiling. Or… you could find small openings at the bottom of the stacks and hide in a cave or crawl through a tunnel. Back then, the feed sacks were made of cotton instead of paper, and they were pretty hard to bust open. If you were a couple of 11-year-olds playing cowboys and Indians, that feed room was full of canyons, mountains, and wonderful ambush sites! I shudder now to think of what could have happened to us if some of those stacks would have fallen over and crushed us. No one even knew we were back there. When we got too hot, there was always the icehouse to cool off in. The entrance to the icehouse was a huge steel door that you opened by lifting a lever, and the door was so heavy it took both of us to pull it open. We would run inside, find a huge block of ice, and see who could sit on one the longest. We would almost freeze our bottoms off before one of us would finally jump up! Here again, it gives me the shivers (pardon the pun) to think what could have happened if someone would have seen that door ajar and pushed it shut, not knowing we were in there. Our favorite time would come when Mr. Yon would let us have our snack at the end of the day. Mr. Thornton, the butcher, would cut us a few slices of cheese and we could each get a free coke, a package of crackers, and a can of Vienna sausage. Back to the feed room we'd go for our "campfire" meal at the end of the day. What kid could have asked for anything better?

Looking back on how many dangerous things I did as a child; I reflect on how my guardian angel must have been exhausted at times. Yes, I truly believe in angels because the Bible tells me they are real.

Matthew 18:10 – "Take heed that ye despise not one of these little ones; for I say unto you, that in heaven their angels do always behold the face of my Father which is in heaven."

Psalm 91:11-12 – "For He shall give His angels charge over you, to keep you in all your ways. In their hands they shall bear you up, lest you dash your foot against a stone."

96

Hero Me

Every kid dreams of being a hero. I know I always did. When I was growing up, there was no shortage of heroes, and we watched them ride across the screen every Saturday at the movie theater. There was Hopalong Cassidy, Roy Rogers, the Lone Ranger, Tarzan, and many more. For only 25 cents, we would sit mesmerized as we watched them rescue people from burning buildings, raging rivers, killer outlaws, and stampedes at the risk of their own lives. I used to lie in bed at night, picturing in my mind the many ways I could be a hero in the face of great danger. Well….one day I got my opportunity.

When I was about 11 years old, I was spending the day with Tommye Hodge, my friend who lived about halfway between Magnolia and Plantersville. Several of her cousins were visiting as well; a boy about my age, and two girls about nine and seven. We hiked down to Hurricane Creek that was about 1/4 mile behind her house, pulled off our shoes, and began splashing in the water. Suddenly, I spied a huge cat track at the edge of the creek bed. It was as big as my hand, but the scariest part was that it was slowly filling up with water, which meant it was pretty fresh. Over across the creek, there was a small pen with a white horse in it, and he had quit grazing and stood watching us play. Suddenly there was a loud scream that sounded like a woman being murdered! The horse ran around in a short circle and then cleared that fence like it wasn't even there. We all looked at each other and began running up the path toward Tommye's house like a bunch of scared rabbits. The youngest girl was up ahead of me, and I saw her stop suddenly and begin to cry. She was barefooted and had run through a patch of grass burrs. Well, this is the part where you should be reading about my heroics, but sad to say, I went flying right by her like she wasn't even there. I mean I didn't even miss a step. I looked back long enough to see that her big brother had stopped to help her, and that was the image I consoled myself with for years to come. She was helped. She didn't get torn apart by a wild panther… but no thanks to me. Some hero I was. As I led the way into Tommye's back yard, we couldn't talk enough about our experience. "Did you hear that scream?" "It had to be a panther!" "Did you see how high that horse jumped over that fence?" The one question I was very glad not to hear was, "Why didn't you stop to help my little sister?" I'll have to say it was a very humbling experience that has remained in my mind all this time. I know…. I was just a kid, and I was scared, yada, yada, yada, but it took me a long time to forgive myself. I sure didn't lie in bed thinking about being a hero anymore.

That experience really influenced the way I began to think of myself as I grew into adulthood, and if, God forbid, I ever have to put myself in danger to help someone else, I pray that God will give me the courage to do whatever is necessary.

Romans 12:3 – "Don't think you are better than you really are. Be honest in your evaluation of yourselves, measuring yourselves by the faith God has given you."

97

Throwing Dick out of the Truck

One day when I was about 13, I was visiting my friend Gaye Yancey. We were playing basketball out behind the garage when her dad came out and said he needed to throw out some hay for his cows. We climbed into his old red pickup and headed for the barn where we helped him toss some bales of hay into the bed, and then Gaye got behind the wheel. She was only 12, but she knew already how to handle that truck.

As she slowly pulled out into the pasture, Dick cut the string from a bale of hay, stood up, and began kicking the hay out of the back of the truck. I called her parents Dick and Juanita, and she called mine Dub and Celeste. Back then, we did that sometimes if the adults didn't care.

Anyway, it wasn't long before I was nagging at her to let me drive. She asked me if I could drive a stick shift, and of course I told her that I had been watching her and it couldn't be too hard. She stopped the truck and as we were walking around to change places Dick asked what we were doing. Gaye told him I was going to drive, and he immediately asked me if I knew how to drive a stick shift. I assured him that I could do it, that it was no problem.

Climbing behind the wheel, I stretched to reach the clutch and could barely see over the steering wheel. For all you people who know how to drive a standard shift, you can probably figure out what happened next. I shoved it into first gear, popped the clutch, and pushed hard on the gas. Immediately the truck began to lurch back and forth, and I heard a yell from the back of the truck. Looking in the rear-view mirror I saw Dick's arms go up in the air and to my horror he disappeared. At first the cows jumped back a little, and then they all began jogging forward to get to the hay. I just knew he was going to be killed…either from being thrown from the truck or run over in a stampede…and if he wasn't, then he was going to kill ME!

Of course, the truck had died so I didn't need to put the brakes on, and Gaye and I jumped out of the truck. As we ran back to drive the cows away and check on her dad, I was scared to look. It was going to be bad. To my great relief, before we even got to the back of the truck Dick had jumped up and was dusting himself off. Also, to my surprise, he was laughing real hard. We just stood there gawking at him, as he was covered in dust and hay, and then we began laughing too. I was so glad that he had a good sense of humor and wasn't mad at me at all. He just told me to let the clutch out slowly when I had it in first gear. I couldn't believe he was going to let me try it again, but I noticed that when he got back in the truck to throw the rest of the hay out, he got down on his knees to do it!

What could have been a bad accident, had turned into something that would become a funny memory. The story was told and retold, and years later it would always bring a smile to our faces when someone would say, "Remember when you threw Dick out of the back of the truck?"

Now that's a funny story, but in looking back I can see the mistake Dick made. He had trusted me when I told him I could drive a stick shift, and he could have suffered serious injury because of it. God tells us that we should never trust what people tell us regarding our salvation without testing it against His Word. The devil delights in deception and uses it to further his own kingdom.

1 John 4:1-3 – "Dear friends, do not believe every spirit, but test the spirits to see whether they are from God, because many false prophets have gone out into the world. This is how you can recognize the Spirit of God: Every spirit that acknowledges that Jesus Christ has come in the flesh is from God, but every spirit that does not acknowledge Jesus is not from God. This is the spirit of the antichrist, which you have heard is coming and even now is already in the world."

Gaye Yancey and me

98
Union Suit

I love history. Guess I learned to love it from hearing my grandparents and Auntie tell me stories of when they were growing up. Picturing in my mind the things they did "back in the old days" just fascinated me. In school, it was my very favorite subject and I always paid close attention in class. How ironic then, that it was in a history class where I first got in trouble at school.

Jimmy Murphy was our junior high basketball coach, and he also taught 7th grade history. Coach Murphy and his wife were close friends with my mom and dad and visited often. I really liked Coach Murphy, and since I also really liked history, you might wonder why I got in trouble. Well…I know all kids say this, but it *really* wasn't my fault.

We were studying the Civil War, and like a lot of people I had ancestors who had fought on both sides, so I was really interested. At home, we all talked about the day's events around the supper table. One night I was telling them about what we were studying in history class and my dad told me to do something. (Keep in mind, my dad was a real practical joker.) He said, "Tomorrow, when you are in your history class, tell Coach Murphy that your great-great grandfather fought for the Confederacy, but he wore a union suit." I thought that was awesome. I figured he must have been a spy or something, and I could hardly wait for our history class to start so I could brag about this in front of my friends. This naïve 12-year-old had no idea that a union suit was just another name for long underwear, or "long handles" as we used to call them.

The next day when Coach Murphy got the class started, I raised my hand and waved it around so he'd be sure to see me. He asked me what I wanted, and with a huge grin on my face I told him, "My great-great grandfather fought for the Confederacy, but he wore a union suit!" I heard a few snickers in the classroom, but Coach just glared at me and said, "Tarvah, I'm surprised at you. That was really uncalled for." Then he told me to go stand out in the hall. That's what we had to do for punishment sometimes… stand out in the hall. It was very embarrassing out there, as teachers would walk by and see you and sometimes the high school kids who had permission to go to the bathroom or something would walk by and make fun of you for being out there. I also knew that my mom would hear about this because her office was right down the hall.

After class was over, I asked Coach Murphy what I had done wrong, and I told him my dad had told me to tell him that in class. Coach got a twinkle in his eye and told me what a union suit really was. I was very embarrassed, but he just laughed and said for me not to worry about it; that it was just intended to be a big joke. The next day he even apologized in front of the class for reprimanding me and explained the situation to the other kids. However, for a very long time after that I cross-examined my dad each time he told me something. After all, he'd really pulled a big one on me!

I learned a valuable lesson back then that I still apply to my life today. Question what others tell us to do, or what they say, even if it's from someone we might trust. False prophets can make a lie seem like the truth, and the only way to know the difference is to ask God and read and study His Word. It's the best way I know of to stay out of trouble!

1 John 4:1 – "Dear friends, do not believe every spirit, but test the spirits to see whether they are from God, because many false prophets have gone out into the world."

1 Thessalonians 5:21 – "Test all things; hold fast that which is good."

Coach Murphy

99
Whispering in Church

In my early growing-up years, First Baptist Church, Magnolia, was very small if you compare it to what it is now, and the congregation got very excited if we had as many as 85 in Sunday School. I always had to sit by my parents until I was about 10, and then I could only sit on the pews that were in front of them where they could keep an eye on me. Brother Gerald Canon was our pastor back then, and he was just 19 when we called him to preach. The church paid his way through Seminary, and I guess that was part of his salary.

We all called him Brother Gerald, and he baptized me when I was only nine years old. Even back then everyone usually sat in the same place every Sunday, and it was easy to see who was absent because their spot was empty. My mom, dad, Jimmy and I sat on the left side on the fifth row. In my mind, I can clearly see where "Little Old Mrs. Ware" used to sit. Second row from the front on the right side as you faced the pulpit, and she sat on the very end toward the stained-glass window. When I was about 10 or 11, my friends and I would sometimes sit in her spot, and when Mrs. Ware came in she would tap our legs with her cane and tell us to get out of her seat. I think she enjoyed it as much as we did though, because she'd always have a little twinkle in her eye.

It wasn't until I got in junior high that I was allowed to sit behind my parents. Oh, this was such freedom! My friends and I could whisper, pass notes, and make faces at each other, but you had to be sure to get on the very back row or someone in the congregation would tell your parents what you were doing. That was *after* they had reached up and tapped you on the shoulder and told you to behave yourself! They didn't mind doing that kind of thing back then. Anyway, I vividly remember one Sunday when Pam Moseley, Joyce Evans, Melba Hosford and I had achieved the very best spot on the back row. We didn't cut up any during the singing part of the service because we all liked to sing, but when the sermon began, so did the note-passing and the whispering.

We could hear Brother Gerald just preaching away in the background as we had our fun, but suddenly everything got really quiet. We glanced up from our "activities" to see Brother Gerald staring at us with a very stern look on his face. Then to our great humiliation he said very slowly, "Tarvah, if you, Pam, Joyce, and Melba will quit whispering and passing your notes around, I'll get on with my sermon." Well…. you could have heard a pin drop, and everyone in the church, including my parents, slowly turned around and looked at us. You can bet your bottom dollar that we hardly moved for the rest of the sermon. We didn't even turn to look at each other, so great was our embarrassment. You can also believe that I got a pretty good chewing out from my parents after church, and it was many Sundays before I was again allowed the "privilege" of sitting on the back row. Our big mistake was in thinking that because everyone was facing the preacher, we wouldn't be seen, but we had overlooked the preacher, himself!

I can apply that same principle to my everyday life now. Nothing I do or say, or think, is in secret. It might be hidden from everyone else, but God sees and knows it all.

Hebrews 4:13 – "Nothing in all creation is hidden from God. Everything is naked and exposed before his eyes, and he is the one to whom we are accountable."

Proverbs 5:21 – "The Lord sees everything you do. Wherever you go, he is watching."

100

Jumping the Hump

Back when I was growing up you could get your driver's license when you were 14 years old. There's a very good reason why that law was changed. Fourteen-year-olds shouldn't be allowed to have complete, unsupervised control of a 4,000 lb. vehicle. Yeah, back then cars weighed that much and more because they were made of steel…not fiberglass. When I was able to obtain my certified driver's license in 1958 at the ripe old age of 14 years and 2 mos., my grandfather had just passed away and we had his 1952 Oldsmobile as a second car. To me, it was like driving a Sherman tank. I had to sit on a pillow to be able to see over the steering wheel, and still had to move the seat forward as far as it would go to reach the gas pedal. That's what we called it back then…a gas pedal. Anyway, it just so happened that FM 1488 was being constructed and it was still in the dirt and gravel stage. Also, since it was built up a little higher than the other roads, there was a hump where S. Goodson crossed it. That's the street that runs in front of where the post office is now located. One day I heard my brother, Jimmy, and some of his friends talking about how much fun it was to "jump the hump." That if you hit it around 25 mph, you'd become a little airborne before hitting the ground on the other side. That sure sounded like a lot of fun, and I couldn't wait to try it. One day, I got permission to drive the car out to Gaye Yancey's house to visit. Here was my big opportunity! However, 25 mph sounded a little too slow to me and a little voice in my head told me it would be a lot more fun if I went a little faster. Approaching 1488, I stretched as high as I could to see over the steering wheel, and pressed down on the gas pedal, hitting the hump at around 35 mph. Amidst a cloud of dust and gravel, the car went sailing into the air. Whump! When I finally came to a landing on the other side, the hood, and the lid of the trunk both popped up in the air, and I began skidding sideways. I couldn't see a thing for the hood in my face! Immediately hitting the brakes, I brought the car to a stop right in the middle of the road. Thankfully, there was hardly any traffic back then, and there were no other cars on the road. On shaky legs, I got out of the car and slammed the hood down, praying that it wasn't broken and would stay latched. It wasn't, and it did. Then I went to the back and shut the trunk. Same result...everything was okay except my nerves. Needless to say, I drove very slowly the rest of the way to Gaye's house.

I learned that day, that there's a huge difference between being adventuresome and being reckless. I also learned that that little voice in my head could sometimes get me in trouble if I listened to it. I'll have to confess that I still "jumped the hump" every chance I got, but from that time on, I did it *verrrry* carefully.

Proverbs 14:16 – "One who is wise is cautious and turns away from evil, but a fool is reckless and careless."

101

Driving Mr. Yon's Car

One of the big advantages of growing up in the country is learning how to drive a car at an early age. It also helps when you have the opportunity to do this in a large pasture where not much can go wrong. Note that I said, "not much!" When I was about 12 years old, the acreage where Magnolia Elementary School now stands was just a large fenced-in pasture belonging to Mr. Yon. His house stood on the corner where a used car lot is now. The only things in that pasture were two small stock ponds that were located at the far corners of the acreage, and Mr. Yon's white horse, Silver. Two of these items played a prominent role in my first driving experience.

Whenever Mr. Yon's niece, Diane, came out to spend some time in Magnolia, we would always get together and play. At the ripe old age of 13, Diane already knew the basics of driving a car and she promised to teach me. Mr. Yon had an old, white Cadillac that stayed parked in the garage behind his house, and he would let Diane practice driving it around in the pasture. One afternoon when she was visiting, she got the car keys and told me it was time that I learned how to drive. So out the back door we went, and I "patiently" waited until she backed the car out and got it pointed toward the middle of the pasture.

When I got in the driver's seat, I had to look under the top rim of the steering wheel to just barely be able to see over the hood, and I had to really stretch to get my toes to touch the accelerator. Let me tell you, that was a BIG car! Well, I put it in drive, and off we went. Immediately, I spied Silver and thought what a lot of fun it would be to "herd" him around the pasture with the car, so I took dead aim and drove slowly toward him. He looked up, saw me coming, and began to trot, which meant that I had to drive a little faster. The faster he went, the faster I went. Too late, I saw that he was heading toward the pond, and when he veered away, I just kept going straight. "Stop! Stop!" Diane was yelling. Frantically, I tried to reach the brake, but my toes slipped off. It didn't help matters that there was mud all around the edge of the pond and by the time I finally hit the brakes we slid until the front tires were totally submerged and the rear tires were in soft mud. Slamming the car in reverse, I stomped on the pedal and mud and water went everywhere. When the tires got some traction, we shot backward out of that pond like a torpedo!

Finally, after what seemed an eternity, I got the car stopped and we sat there shaking and scared. The car was a mess, with mud and dirty water spots all over it, so we decided we'd better wash it. I parked it behind the garage where no one would see us and we scrubbed it from top to bottom. Diane carefully parked the car back in the garage and we hoped we were safe from discovery. We didn't even think about the ruts we left down by the pond. I never knew if Mr. Yon found out about our little incident, but I know he must have seen those ruts, and wondered how his car got so clean. If he ever said anything to my parents, I never knew that either. I guess sometimes adults actually remember that they were kids once too.

Many times in our lives we think that if no one knows about a wrong thing we did, we can just go on like it didn't happen. However, there is One who sees and knows everything we do, and He will hold us accountable for the times we disobey Him.

Hebrews 4:13 – "Nothing in all creation is hidden from God's sight. Everything is uncovered and laid bare before the eyes of him to whom we must give account."

102

Basketball Shoes

There are two facts that describe my 7th grade year in junior high school. One… I had a passion for basketball. Two… I was only 4'4" tall. Now for those of you who follow the sport, you understand what I'm talking about. When the goal is 8' off the ground and you're that short, the game presents a real challenge. That didn't stop me though because I just worked harder than everyone else. After every practice I would stay on the court practicing free throws, dribbling, and layups. I can't really brag about having a good work ethic, because practice was enjoyable for me, and I just had fun doing it.

Magnolia was a small school at that time, and we had to combine the 7th and 8th grades to have one junior high team. Back then, we played half-court basketball with three forwards and three guards on each end of the court. All my hard work paid off when Coach Murphy made me a starting forward on the "B" team. I was little, but I could run fast and if I got ahead of my guard there was no one to block my layups. There was one very memorable game for me that year, and it happened to be an "away" game. About half-way to our game, I discovered I had left my tennis shoes back at the gym. We were all issued those white, high-top Converse tennis shoes with our uniforms. In those days, all the girls wore dresses, or skirts and blouses to the games, and our shoes were either loafers, flats, or oxfords. Gosh, how was I going to tell Coach Murphy that I didn't have my tennis shoes? Everyone was singing those dumb songs we all sang on the school bus (99 bottles of beer on the wall, etc.), and I was usually one of the loudest. But how can you sing when you're sick at your stomach? When we got to our destination, everyone got their gear and began getting off the bus and I stopped Coach Murphy and told him what I had done. He got pretty upset and told me that my carelessness had not only let him down but had let my team down as well. I went into the gym with all the others and was sitting dejectedly on the bench while they began to warm up, when suddenly I saw Coach Murphy walking toward me with a pair of tennis shoes in his hands. He had explained my predicament to the opposing coach who had come up with a pair of tennis shoes just my size. I can't tell you who won the game that day, I just remember the elation I felt when I found out I was going to be able to play! I can also tell you that I never forgot my tennis shoes again!

This little episode in my life provides a very good lesson for me today. I can't be one of God's players by sitting on the bench. If I'm going to be an active member of His team, I must be totally prepared, with a complete uniform, to overcome the challenges and temptations of this world.

Ephesians 6:13 – "Therefore put on the full armor of God, so that when the day of evil comes, you may be able to stand your ground, and after you have done everything, to stand."

103

Reading in the Band Hall

Most of you know by now that I really love to read. I always have. Sometimes I get really lost in a book and can't put it down until I finish it. That particular trait got me in a lot of trouble when I was a freshman in high school.

I played in the Magnolia High School band, and had worked up to 1st chair, 3rd clarinet. That meant that I sat on the third row of a semicircle around the band director's podium, and I sat in the first chair on that row. Don Jeter was our band director, and he demanded that we work hard and do our very best. Well, one day I was close to finishing a really good book, and I got this neat idea. Since my row was pretty far away from the director's podium, I decided to place the open book on my music stand and finish reading it while pretending to play the music. My good friend, Pam Moseley, sat right by me, and I knew she'd never tell on me. Anyway, I got really involved in the story and didn't notice when the band stopped playing. There I sat, with my clarinet still up to my mouth, and the first thing I noticed was a big hand reaching over the top of the music stand grabbing my book. Mr. Jeter picked up my book, and with a mighty backhand, threw it clear across the band hall, hitting the wall. Whap! It sounded like a bomb going off. You could have heard a pin drop in the band hall. "Graves!" (Mr. Jeter always called you by your last name when you were in trouble.) "Do you think you're so good that you don't have to practice like the rest of the band?" "No, sir," I barely breathed. "Do you want to be the one that costs us a "1" in concert at UIL because of a stupid mistake?" he shouted, "Do you want to be the one that lets everyone down after they've worked hard?" "No, sir," I said quietly while looking at the floor. "Well, you can just stay after school and make up for the practice time that you've missed. You don't need to leave until you get it right!" I was really glad when he turned around and went back to the podium and I was no longer the object of his wrath.

That after-school session was very memorable, to say the least, but I worked hard and I got it right. I can look back at that time now, and really appreciate how Mr. Jeter brought out the best in all of us and we worked hard to make him proud.

I'm so thankful that I don't need to work hard to get into Heaven, because Jesus took care of that for me. However, I don't want to be ashamed when I get there either. We only have one shot at living the life He wants us to live here on earth. I sure hope I get it right.

2 Timothy 2:15 (NIV) – "Study to shew thyself approved unto God, a workman that needeth not to be ashamed, rightly dividing the word of truth."

104

Hank Mostyn's Broken Arm

I really love horses. I always have. Although I never had one of my own, many of my friends had horses so I was always able to enjoy horseback riding when I was growing up. Most of my memories involving those rides are really happy ones, but there was one time that I would like to be able to put out of my mind.

When I was about 13, I went to spend the day with Jody Mostyn, one of my best friends, and we decided to go fishing. The place we wanted to go was a little distance from the house, so we thought that it would be fun to ride the horses down there. As we were saddling up, her little brother, Hank, who was in elementary school, came over and begged to tag along. Hurriedly, I threw the saddle on his horse, Sugarfoot, and off we went with our rods and reels. Funny, I can remember his horse's name, but not the names of the ones we rode.

Later, on the way home, Jody and I thought it would be fun to race our horses, so we gave our tackle to Hank to hold. Off we went, with not even a thought in mind that Sugarfoot would want to run too. Of course, he took off right behind us, and here came Hank, one hand full of rods and reels, and the other hand on the reins. He might have been okay, if not for one little important thing. The cinch slipped. The first we knew of it was when we heard him yell. As we looked around, we could see him sitting on the ground with one arm draped over his leg. He was holding that arm and crying. I immediately thought he had fallen off and stuck a fishing lure in his arm, but when we got to him it was very obvious that something even worse had happened, and his arm was broken in two places just above his wrist. He was sitting there, Indian style, crying, and his broken arm was just lying across one of his legs. I'll never forget that sight as long as I live.

I happened to glance over at Sugarfoot and thought I was going to be sick. There he stood, with the saddle hanging over on his side. In my haste to get him saddled, I hadn't thought to make sure he hadn't swelled up as horses do most of the time. If I had only taken the time to do the job right! This was all my fault! Jody got on her horse and raced to the house to get her dad while I stayed with Hank.

Pretty soon, Mr. Mostyn drove up in the pickup and jumped out. Right off the bat, he saw Sugarfoot and immediately demanded to know who had saddled that horse! It was the hardest thing in the world to tell him that I had done it. He just looked at me and, much to his credit, he didn't say another thing about it. We got Hank back to the house and off they went with him to the hospital, while I called my mom to come get me. But just before they left, I heard Mrs. Mostyn say that they wouldn't be able to put Hank to sleep to fix his arm because at an earlier time when he had been put under, he had stopped breathing. My thought then was, "Oh my gosh. I could have killed him," and all because I was in a hurry and did a sloppy job.

I learned a valuable lesson that day. Sometimes it's not always me that suffers the consequences of my carelessness…. sometimes someone else gets hurt, and that's even worse.

Colossians 3:23 – "And whatsoever ye do, do it heartily, as to the Lord, and not unto men."

Me and Jody Mostyn about the time of Hank's accident

105

Rotten Eggs

My dad grew up in China Spring, Texas, a small town just a little northwest of Waco, and my grandparents lived there until they passed away. It was always an adventure to go see them. My aunt, uncle, and cousins lived in Waco so we would all get together while we were there. My cousin, David, was about a year older than me, and we always found something interesting to do. Big Daddy and Big Mama had chickens and ducks, and there was a big barn right behind their house.

On one memorable trip when I was about 9 years old, David and I climbed up in the loft and discovered a nest of duck eggs with about 10 eggs still in it. Most of the time, we played cowboys and Indians, but this kind of ammunition called for war! Immediately dividing up the eggs, we split up and began stalking each other. Let me tell you, those eggs made great grenades! After the first couple of "explosions" we discovered that the eggs were rotten, but that made it even more fun, especially when you scored a near hit! Pretty soon, we heard our parents calling us to come in and get ready to go home. Hurriedly, we ran to the water hose and washed the mess off before we went inside. The first words we heard were, "What in the world have y'all been up to?" "What is that awful smell?" Then we realized that we hadn't been able to get the smell off our clothes (and probably out of our hair) so there was no need to do anything but tell the truth. Needless to say, we were in BIG trouble, and after the chewing out we were sent back outside to stay until it was time to go home. Let me tell you, that was one, long ride back to Magnolia and it was hardly bearable even with the windows down. When we got home, I had to scrub from the top of my head to the tip of my toes, but it sure felt good to get clean again!

Sin is a lot like those rotten duck eggs. It might seem like fun at the time, but there will always be consequences. You can try to hide it and cover it up, but the stain and aftereffects linger on and make you miserable. Generally, the people around you suffer too. I still remember how wonderful it was when I found out that God would forgive my sins and that Jesus would wash them away. How good it felt to be clean again!

"Sin had left a crimson stain…. He washed it white as snow."

First Verse I Memorized

A while back, our pastor spent a few weeks encouraging us to commit scripture verses to memory and it made me think of the first verse I ever memorized. Most people start out with John 3:16, but that wasn't the first one I learned.

Papaw (W. J. Gayle) had been a deacon at First Baptist Church Magnolia since long before I could remember, and when he prayed aloud in church, he always ended his prayer this way: "Let the words of my mouth, and the meditation of my heart, be acceptable in thy sight oh Lord my strength and my redeemer. Amen." So, Psalm 19:14 was the first verse I ever memorized although I didn't realize at the time that it was from the Bible. I just thought it was something Papaw always said when he prayed.

Papaw had a lot of Irish blood in him, and like most Irishmen, he had a quick temper and was a "little" impulsive. I'm sure this was his cross to bear in life, so he probably felt he needed to hold this verse in his heart and think of it often. Papaw never, ever, cursed, but he knew that words spoken in anger, or without thinking, could create damaging wounds that might never be completely healed. He also knew that he needed God's help to deal with this all his life. I believe there was a reason for this being the first verse I ever learned, as I, too, have needed it in my heart every day.

Pap went to live with the Lord when I was in the eighth grade, but I can still picture him (yes, I peeped when we were supposed to have our heads bowed and eyes closed) standing in church, praying, and saying:

Psalm 19:14 – "Let the words of my mouth, and the meditation of my heart, be acceptable in thy sight oh Lord my strength and my redeemer."

*Papaw, about the time
I memorized the verse*

Cursed at School

One Sunday, our pastor, Brother Ed, preached the last sermon in a series entitled "Speech Therapy" and it reminded me of an unpleasant incident in my childhood.

"I just said a curse word," I thought to myself! Oh my gosh, it had just slipped out. I was playing tag at recess with my third-grade friends, and in the midst of all the excitement of the game… I said it. I didn't really mean to say it. Actually It was just a combination of two of my favorite slang words, "good grief" and "gosh dog" but it came out "G.. dog!" My friends immediately stopped playing and stared at me. "You just cussed, and I'm gonna tell!" one of the kids said. I immediately felt sick at my stomach. Gosh, what was my teacher going to think? "Don't tell her," I begged. "It just slipped out. I didn't mean to say it." Even worse… what was my mom going to think? At that time, Mom was secretary to the superintendent of schools, and all twelve grades and the administration offices were on the same campus. That meant that Mom was not very far away, and I knew that the teacher would tell her before I had a chance to confess to her myself. Well, as it turned out, I talked the kid into not telling my teacher, but I was still sick at heart the rest of the day. Most of that afternoon was spent with me trying to figure out how to tell my mom that I had taken God's name in vain right there in front of all the other kids. When school was over, my mom could tell something wasn't right the minute I got in the car. "What's wrong, Tarvah? Are you sick?" she asked. I managed to mumble that I was okay, but as soon as we got home, I jumped out of the car and as I ran toward the house, I said, "Mom, meet me in the bathroom." Now if you've read my stories before, you understand that the bathroom was our "confessional." Mom would sit on the edge of the bathtub, and I would sit on the toilet lid, and I'd tell her everything. Well, I closed the door, we took our places, and I told her what had happened. "Mom, I cussed on the playground today," I blurted out. She just looked at me for a minute and then asked me what happened. When I finished telling her, she said, "Tarvah, I know you really didn't mean to say that, and God knows it too." "He does?" I asked her. "Yes, He does, but He still wants you to tell him you're sorry," she said. "It hurts God's heart when you use His name that way." With a sigh of relief, I told her I'd already done that, right after I said it. "Do you still love me?" I asked her, "And does God still love me?" She just smiled, gave me a big hug and told me, "Of course I do, and God does too. Just be very careful not to do it again." What a huge relief! I was still loved, and all was right with my world again!

Looking back on that incident, I realize that even though my words weren't intentional, all the kids that heard me say them didn't know that. Now, every day I need to start the day with this scripture: "Let the words of my mouth, and the meditation of my heart, be acceptable in thy sight, oh Lord my strength and my redeemer" (Psalm 19:14).

108

Carving Soap

One dreary, rainy day, my brother and I were moaning and groaning about what a boring day it was. There was just nothing for a twelve-year-old and a seven-year-old to do except fuss and argue with each other. After listening to us gripe and fuss for a while, Daddy finally said, "I know something you can do!" He then proceeded to lay some newspaper pages on the floor, and while Jimmy and I stood there wondering what he was up to, he went into the bathroom and came back with two large bars of Ivory soap. Placing them on the newspaper, he then went to the kitchen and brought back two, small paring knives. As we just looked at him with frowns on our faces, he handed each of us a knife and said, "Why don't you carve something out of the soap?" Wow! What a great idea! We quickly sat down Indian style by the newspaper and began unwrapping the soap. "Be very careful with the knives, and don't cut yourselves," Daddy said. "Take your time because you have all day." While Jimmy sat there thinking about what he wanted to carve, I picked up my bar of soap and quickly started my project. I knew exactly what I wanted to make.... a horse! The Ivory soap was flaky and very ease to carve, so I immediately started to work. First, I carved out the head and made some eyes and a mouth. The ears were a little tricky, and I had a problem getting them the same size. I finally got the head finished, and the neck wasn't too hard, but then the difficult part began. I had a large square of soap that needed to have legs and tail carved out. I thought getting two ears evenly matched was hard but getting four legs the same size was a real challenge! I seemed to keep cutting too far up into the body with one leg or the other. Before too long I had a horse that was all legs and tail, with a very small body and a huge head. This presented a real problem. I decided I needed to make the head smaller, and maybe cut the legs a little shorter. So, I cut some off the bottom of each leg, and a little off the tail. Patiently, I carved the head smaller, but as I concentrated on shaping the ears, I gripped the body a little too hard and the two back legs snapped off. Oh, no! Well.... there I sat, with only a funny-looking lump of soap in my hand. That was all that was left after a whole

211

afternoon of hard work! As I sat there, dejected, I again heard Daddy's voice. "Don't worry, Tarvah. You'll do better next time. It just takes practice. In the meantime, we can still use the soap."

I did get better the next time, and I also learned a lesson. Be very patient and careful with whatever you're working on, and never throw away the unfinished product! I'm so thankful that God is that way with us!

Isaiah 64:8 – "But now, O Lord, You are our Father, We are the clay, and You our potter; And all of us are the work of Your hand."

2 Peter 3:9 – "The Lord is not slow about His promise, as some count slowness, but is patient toward you, not wishing for any to perish but for all to come to repentance."

109

Kite of Many Colors

Back in the day, when I was growing up in Magnolia, kite flying was a popular and fun pastime for kids. At the ripe old age of six I really wanted a kite of my own, and I knew just where I could fly it…. on the vacant lot across from the Methodist Church. The problem was, Mr. Yon didn't have kites for sale in his store. You had to go all the way to Tomball to get one.

Well, one day I was visiting Papaw, who lived just one block over and down from the church, and I asked him if he would take me to Tomball and buy me a kite. Papaw said, "Tarvah, I won't take you to Tomball, but I'll make you a kite." What? He could make a kite? Of course, being a kid and being impatient, I asked him if he'd make it right then. He told me it would take a couple of days, but he'd get right on it. Papaw had a small workshop behind his house where he enjoyed building things and tinkering with things that needed fixing, so he went out there and began cutting small strips of wood for a kite frame. The frame had to be light enough and thin enough for the wind to lift it, but still strong enough to hold up against the wind. But Papaw knew just how to do that. The measurements had to be just right for it to be balanced. But Papaw knew how to do that too. After the frame was finished, he glued all the pieces together and set it aside to dry. Then I asked him, "Papaw, what are you going to use for the material?" Just giving me a little smile, he left the workshop and went to the house, with me following right behind. Inside, he picked up the Sunday newspaper, took out the brightly colored comics section, grabbed a pair of scissors, a jar of glue, an old scrap of white cloth, and headed back out to the workshop. Placing the comics over the frame, Papaw began to trim the pages to fit. I wondered how he was going to make all the sections stay on the frame, but again, Papaw knew just how to do that. Opening the jar of glue, he began to fasten the trimmed pieces to the frame, gluing each piece firmly in place. As I stood there frowning, wondering what was coming next, he picked up the cloth and began to cut it into strips….one very long piece, and several small pieces. "This will be the kite's tail," he said, and he began to tie the small pieces around the long piece at short intervals. "Now, we have to wait until tomorrow for the glue to dry, and then we'll fly your kite," Papaw told me.

Tomorrow finally arrived, and we took the kite to the vacant lot across from the Methodist Church. Papaw carefully attached the tail to the bottom of the frame and tied one end of a long cord of string to the crossbar of the frame. Holding the kite high over his head, he told me to walk away, playing out the kite string until he yelled at me to stop. Then he said, "Run, Tarvah, and fly your kite!" I ran as hard as I could and felt a tug on the end of the string. I turned around, and there it was…. flying high in the air! The sun was shining through those colored comics, and it was the prettiest kite I ever saw, with a long white tail flowing in the wind! That scene is forever etched in my memory. My kite was not only beautiful….it was the only one like it in the whole world…and it was all mine!

Remembering Papaw building my kite reminds me of our own creation. God created man in His own image, but like my homemade kite, each of us is unique and different in our own way. And like my kite gave me joy, we, as God's own creation, are very special to Him!

Matthew 10:30 – "But even the hairs of your head are all numbered."

Psalm 139:14 – "I praise you, for I am fearfully and wonderfully made. Wonderful are your works; my soul knows it very well."

Ephesians 2:10 – "For we are his workmanship, created in Christ Jesus for good works, which God prepared beforehand, that we should walk in them."

110

Lesson of the Iron

Some lessons are much more painful than others. I received such a lesson when I was about nine years old.

"Mom! I can do that! Let me do it!" I was watching my mom iron Daddy's handkerchiefs, and it looked like fun to me. She would smooth out the handkerchief and lightly sprinkle it from a water bottle with a cork sprinkler stuck in the top. "Tarvah… it's not as easy as you think. The iron is very hot, and you must be careful, or you'll burn yourself. You can also scorch the handkerchief," she said. "I'll be careful. I promise," I told her. So, that was how it began.

There were about ten handkerchiefs piled up on the end of the ironing board, so I picked one up and spread it out. After sprinkling it lightly, I began my project. Oops! I left the iron on it too long! Horrified, I gazed down at a dark brown shape on that white handkerchief in the perfect image of an iron. Quickly looking up to see if my mom saw it, I was relieved to see her smile. "See, you can't leave the iron on it too long, or that will happen. Be more careful next time."

After the next five or six handkerchiefs, I had become an expert in my own mind. "This is a snap," I thought to myself. That's when it happened…. the painful lesson that I will try to blame on my brother, Jimmy. He had been watching all that time and was getting a little bored, so he started making faces at me. I was looking at him and holding the iron in my hand, upside down, with the bottom of it facing the ceiling when he made one of his goofiest faces. As I laughed at him, I became very careless with the iron, and it fell back towards me with the bottom of it landing on the inside of my forearm. "Ow!", I screamed, as I quickly threw the iron to the floor. Horrified, and in terrible pain, I looked at the burn on my arm and began sobbing. Grabbing me in her arms, my mom hugged me tight and then led me to the kitchen where she promptly put ice on the burn. Then she applied some ointment, and I saw a bubble about the size of a silver dollar begin to form. Nothing had ever hurt so bad! When the pain had finally subsided a little, my mom gently said, "Tarvah, I warned you to be very careful or you would burn yourself. Now do you understand?" As I tearfully nodded my head, I assured myself that this would never happen again. After about two weeks the burn healed and the scab fell off, leaving a huge scar that didn't disappear until I was around thirteen or fourteen years old. It was a constant reminder of my carelessness.

As I think back on that time, I realize that God allows us to make mistakes in order to teach us to pay attention to His Word and to heed His warning. Oh, how much pain and heartache we could avoid if we obeyed Him.

Hebrews 12:11 – "No discipline seems pleasant at the time, but painful. Later on, however, it produces a harvest of righteousness and peace for those who have been trained by it."

Deuteronomy 8:11 – "But that is the time to be careful! Beware that in your plenty you do not forget the Lord your God and disobey his commands, regulations, and decrees that I am giving you today."

111

The Bookmobile

Kids today probably don't even know what a bookmobile is, but by the time I was in fourth grade the bookmobile was one of the most important things in my life. At that time, I was really into reading the Black Stallion series by Walter Farley and could hardly wait to read the next book. The only library we had was in the high school building and it was for older kids. We didn't have a "city" library then either, so us little kids depended on the bookmobile for our reading material.

I had two major problems with the bookmobile: one was that it only came to the school every two weeks, and the other was that there was a limit on how many books you could check out. The younger classes always got to check out books first, and by the time our class was called I was chomping at the bit! I remember waiting for one particular book, "The Black Stallion and Satan." Satan was the Black's son. In this book he was going to race against his father, and I could hardly wait to see who would win. Well, for some reason the bookmobile never seemed to have that particular book, or some other kid that was reading the same series had already checked it out before I got there. Talk about frustration! Kids today are so lucky. Any time they want to read a book, all they have to do is get it instantly on their Kindle or iPad and read to their heart's content. But it wasn't that way for me! Let me tell you it's hard to wait two weeks, and sometimes four, to read the book you want. When I was finally able to check it out, I think it only took me two days to read it and then the waiting began all over again for the next book. Yes, the bookmobile was one of the most important things in my life, but I guess you could say we had a "love-hate" relationship!

Now I own a book that has no sequel. I don't have to wait for the next "installment." It is complete, and it tells the whole story from beginning to end. It is filled with adventure and has the answers to every question I have. It provides me wisdom, direction, strength, comfort, joy, and total peace. My favorite book of all time—"The Holy Bible."

2 Timothy 3:16-17 – "All Scripture is breathed out by God and profitable for teaching, for reproof, for correction, and for training in righteousness, that the man of God may be competent, equipped for every good work."

Psalm 119:105 – "Thy word is a lamp unto my feet, and a light unto my path."

112

Quite a Kick

At the ripe old age of twelve, I already knew more about horses than Mr. Hodge did. At least that's the thought that went through my mind when he told me to be careful around Robin.

I had gone over to Tommye Hodge's house to spend the afternoon, and we were going horseback riding. They owned two geldings; a gentle black one, and a tall, rawboned sorrel named Robin. Robin wasn't much to look at, but I liked to ride him because he had a lot of spunk. We had just finished eating lunch and were on our way out the door when Mr. Hodge asked, "Where are you girls headed off to?" "We're going to ride the horses down to the creek," Tommye told him. "Who's riding Robin," Mr. Hodge asked. "I am," I told him. "Well, you be careful around him. He likes to nip, and he'll kick you if you aren't careful," he told me. Robin was Mr. Hodge's personal horse, so I should have known that he knew what he was talking about, but I had ridden Robin a few times before and he and I were friends. Mr. Hodge just didn't understand about our relationship. I knew he wouldn't do anything like that to me.

Slamming the kitchen door on our way out, we raced down to the barn and began saddling the horses. Robin was a pretty big horse, and even though I was twelve years old I was only about 4' 6" tall and it was a struggle for me to get him saddled. I hooked the off stirrup onto the horn and shoved the saddle up on his back, then began to make my way to the other side to let the stirrup down. That's when I made my mistake. Instead of just ducking under his neck, I decided to walk around his rear end. Well, you can guess what happened next. Suddenly I felt something like a cannonball hit the side of my left thigh and I went sailing through the air. The next thing I knew, Tommye was standing over me asking if I was okay. "Was I okay?" What was she thinking? Of course, I wasn't okay. I couldn't feel my left leg, so I was certain that Robin had kicked it clear off! It wasn't long though before the feeling began to come back and I knew it was there all right. Boy, did it hurt! Tommye helped me stand up, and as I started limping around, she said, "Dad told you to watch out for that. You should have drug your hand around his hips and walked up close so he couldn't kick you." Well… I didn't need to hear any more advice, so I just glared at her.

Since we were in the barn, out of sight, I began to pull my jeans down to see if there were any bones sticking out. Thankfully, there was just a huge red mark, but it was already beginning to turn purple. As I pulled my jeans back up, Tommye asked me if I still wanted to go riding. Did I want to go riding? Of course, I did! Nothing short of a world-wide disaster would keep me from riding a horse when I had the opportunity. Although the pain in my leg slowed me down a little bit, we finished saddling up and spent the rest of the day riding up and down the creek, running the horses through the water. Later that afternoon when we were finished riding, I swore Tommye to secrecy. "Don't you dare tell your dad that Robin kicked me," I told her, "Because he might not let me ride him anymore." To my knowledge, she never told her dad, because I spent many more happy days on his back. However, I learned a very painful lesson that day, and you can be sure that I never made that mistake again… with Robin, or with any other horse.

It seems I spent a lot of my "growing up" time learning things the hard way… sometimes the painful way.

Proverbs 8:33 – "Heed instruction and be wise, and do not neglect it."

Proverbs 4:10 – "Hear, my son, and accept my sayings, and the years of your life will be many."

Luke 11:28 – "He replied, 'Blessed rather are those who hear the word of God and obey it.'"

113

Lesson of the Muffler

Back in the late 1950's, you could get your driver's license when you were only 14. That's just plain crazy! What 14-year-old has enough sense to be turned loose with a 4,000 lb. torpedo on wheels? Definitely not me, but that's just the way it was. My friend, Gaye, was a year or so younger than me but she could drive as good, or better, than I could, and her dad had a neat pickup that he would let us drive. We'd just cruise up and down the road in front of her house with the windows down, trying to look "cool."

Then one day when I went out to her house, she told me she had discovered something fun and couldn't wait to show me. We got in the pickup and started down the road. As we were driving along she took her foot off the accelerator, reached over and turned off the ignition switch and turned it back on real fast. "Ka-BOOM!" I never heard such a loud noise! "Wow, let me do it!" I said eagerly. Up and down the road we went, backfiring that old pickup over and over again. It was like the 4th of July and New Year's Eve all rolled into one, and right at our fingertips. "Ka-BOOM!" "Ka-*POW!*" I never had so much fun!

And then her dad came home. Getting out of his truck in the driveway, he stood there with his hands on his hips waiting for us to park the truck. "What in the world do you two think you're doing?" he asked. "Don't you know you can blow holes in the muffler when you do that?" No, we didn't know that. We were just having fun. We had no idea it would hurt anything or cause any problems. We were just playing around having fun. "I think you girls just need to park the pickup and find something else to do," he said quietly. Dick was like that. He never chewed us out for anything we did wrong, but he had a way of making us feel bad about it. I found out later that we had blown several holes in the muffler, and he had to buy a new one. What we had considered great fun had cost him some money. He could have made us do some odd jobs around the place and earn the money ourselves, but he didn't do that. He just paid it all himself.

There's another One who did that. He just stepped up and paid the full price for everything we have ever done wrong, and all we have to do is accept that gift.

John 2:2 – "He is the atoning sacrifice for our sins, and not only for ours but also for the sins of the whole world."

Postscript

Just for the record, I would like to add one last story on how the second half of my life's trip began. There would be many more stories and adventures to come…. but that would take another book!

I'll never forget the first time I saw my future husband. I was a very immature 14-year-old high school freshman at Magnolia High School, and he was a newly-hired football coach right out of college. Gosh, Coach McGinty was so good looking! He wore his black hair in a California-style flat-top (short on top with hair combed back on the sides) and since he had been an All-American running back in college, he was in great shape. He also happened to teach driver's education, which I took the second semester of that year. I made it a point to sit on the front row!

Well, on the first day of class I got in trouble. We were doing some work at our desks, and wanting to show off and get attention, I wadded up a sheet of notebook paper and threw it at the waste basket in the corner of the room. The paper hit the wall over the wastebasket, ricocheted off the other wall and rolled out into the middle of the floor. He just looked at me for a while, and then said, "Okay young lady…you owe me a five-page theme tomorrow." Being the shy little girl that I was (hahaha), I quickly said, 'How about double or nothing? If I don't hit it this time, I'll do 10 pages, but if it goes in, I don't have to write anything." He just nodded and said, "Go ahead." I missed again! Then, having no sense at all, I suggested one last try, and with a little smile on his face he told me to go for it. Again, the stupid paper bounced off the wall and I wound up owing him a 20-page theme, but at least he gave me two days to do it. I CAN say, I made an "A" in that class, so he can't complain today about the way I drive!

That first year he coached, he became friends with my mom, who was the superintendent's secretary, and began visiting my parents at our home. My mom and dad liked to play pinochle, but you needed four people to play so they taught me how and I became Coach McGinty's playing partner. I guess you could say that was the beginning of the REAL partnership! Then I began to tag along when they went to movies or ate out. Back in the day the cars were big and had no middle console, so Ginty sat in the front seat with my parents, and I sat in the back. By the end of my sophomore year, he decided to sit in the back seat with me so it wouldn't be so crowded. (Right!) You can be sure I didn't object! It wasn't too long after that, that "Coach McGinty" became "Ginty."

To make a long story a little shorter, we wound up getting married during the summer between my junior and senior year of high school. I had to quit basketball and band because of school rules, and even had to get permission from the school board to attend school so I could graduate. I took some correspondence classes so that I would only have to go to school for one-half day.

The tongues around Magnolia wagged a little bit, spreading a few rumors that we had to get married, but after a year had passed with no baby, the rumors were laid to rest. Our first child was born three years later. Most people also said it would only last a couple of years, but we sure fooled them! After 61 years, two pretty great kids, and a wonderful grandson, we have proved them wrong. The life we share with each other as partners, friends, lovers, and sometimes even competitors (hahaha!) is very special, and we've had a great trip together. We're like the Energizer Bunny… we just keep going and going!

Mark 10:7-9 – "For this cause shall a man leave his father and mother, and cleave to his wife; and they twain shall be one flesh: so then they are no more twain, but one flesh. What therefore God hath joined together, let not man put asunder."

The "pinochle" years

The "engagement" year

The "golden" years

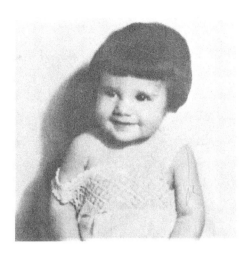 

About the Author

Tarvah Graves McGinty was born on a U.S. Naval Base in Coronado, California (outside of San Diego), on October 9, 1944, to James Willis (Dub) Graves, Jr., and Celeste Graves. However, she got to Magnolia, Texas as soon as she could, at the age of five months old. She returned to California when Dub was called back into the service for the Korean War and started first grade in El Cajon. Within a couple of months, she returned to Magnolia and re-enrolled in first grade. Growing up in Magnolia, Texas, during those years was a wonderful time of innocence, and Tarvah enjoyed the freedom of roaming the town from a very young age. Tarvah married her high school teacher/coach, Gayle McGinty (Ginty), in June 1961, the summer before her senior year. After receiving permission from the school board, she finished her education and graduated from Magnolia High School in 1962. Tarvah began her career as an elementary P.E. aide with Magnolia ISD in 1973, later becoming principal's secretary at Bear Branch Elementary School. She retired from Magnolia ISD in 2000, after serving as secretary to the superintendent of schools for over 15 years. Tarvah and Ginty continued to live in Magnolia, where they raised their two children, Shelley and Ty. Shelley and Ty both graduated from Magnolia High School, and their grandson, Cody, graduated from Magnolia West High School. Cody was the fifth generation to attend Magnolia Schools. Tarvah and Ginty continue to call Magnolia, Texas, their home, and are enjoying their retirement years traveling, hiking, and playing golf together.

Made in the USA
Coppell, TX
26 April 2023

16082703R00129